KNIME Essentials

Perform accurate data analysis using the power
of KNIME

Gábor Bakos

PUBLISHING

BIRMINGHAM - MUMBAI

KNIME Essentials

First published: October 2013

Production Reference: 1101013

Published by Packt Publishing Ltd.
Livery Place
35 Livery Street
Birmingham B3 2PB, UK.

ISBN 978-1-84969-921-1

www.packtpub.com

Cover Image by Abhishek Pandey (abhishek.pandey1210@gmail.com)

Credits

Author
Gábor Bakos

Reviewers
Thorsten Meinl
Takeshi Nakano

Acquisition Editors
Saleem Ahmed
Edward Gordon

Commissioning Editor
Amit Ghodake

Technical Editors
Iram Malik
Aman Preet Singh

Copy Editors
Gladson Monteiro
Kirti Pai
Mradula Hegde
Sayanee Mukherjee

Project Coordinator
Esha Thakker

Proofreader
Clyde Jenkins

Indexers
Tejal Daruwale
Priya Subramani

Graphics
Ronak Dhruv
Yuvraj Mannari

Production Coordinator
Prachali Bhiwandkar

Cover Work
Prachali Bhiwandkar

About the Author

Gábor Bakos is a programmer and a mathematician, having a few years of experience with KNIME and KNIME node development (HiTS nodes and RapidMiner integration for KNIME).

In Trinity College, Dublin, the author was helping a research group with his data analysis skills (also had the opportunity to improve those), and with the new KNIME node development. When he worked for the evopro Kft. or the Scriptum Informatika Zrt., he was also working on various data analysis software products. He currently works for his own company, Mind Eratosthenes Kft. (www.mind-era.com), where he develops the RapidMiner integration for KNIME (tech.knime.org/community/rapidminer-integration), among other things.

The author would like to thank the reviewers and Packt Publishing for their help in creating this book.

About the Reviewers

Thorsten Meinl is currently a Senior Software Developer at KNIME.com in Zurich. He holds a PhD in Computer Science from the University of Konstanz. He has been working on KNIME for over seven years. His main responsibilities are quality assurance, testing, and the continuous integration infrastructure, as well as managing the KNIME Community Contributions. Besides this, he is also interested in parallel computing and cheminformatics.

Takeshi Nakano is a Senior Research Engineer working for Recruit Technologies Co., Ltd. and leads the Advanced Technology Lab in Japan. He holds a Master's degree from the Nara Institute of Science and Technology (NAIST) in Computer Science. He is the lead author of Hadoop Hacks, a book from O'Reilly Japan, and also the author of Getting Started with Apache Solr, a book from GijutsuHyohron in Japan. He loves to find inspiration for his hobbies (reading, scuba diving, and others).

www.PacktPub.com

Support files, eBooks, discount offers and more

You might want to visit www.PacktPub.com for support files and downloads related to your book.

Did you know that Packt offers eBook versions of every book published, with PDF and ePub files available? You can upgrade to the eBook version at www.PacktPub.com and as a print book customer, you are entitled to a discount on the eBook copy. Get in touch with us at service@packtpub.com for more details.

At www.PacktPub.com, you can also read a collection of free technical articles, sign up for a range of free newsletters and receive exclusive discounts and offers on Packt books and eBooks.

http://PacktLib.PacktPub.com

Do you need instant solutions to your IT questions? PacktLib is Packt's online digital book library. Here, you can access, read and search across Packt's entire library of books.

Why Subscribe?

- Fully searchable across every book published by Packt
- Copy and paste, print and bookmark content
- On demand and accessible via web browser

Free Access for Packt account holders

If you have an account with Packt at www.PacktPub.com, you can use this to access PacktLib today and view nine entirely free books. Simply use your login credentials for immediate access.

Table of Contents

Preface

Dear reader, welcome to an intuitive way of data analysis. Using a visual programming language based on dataflows, you can create an easy-to-understand analysis process, while it internally checks signals about some of the common problems. Obviously, any environment that does not help with proper documentation would be destined to fail, but KNIME's success is based not just on its high quality—cross-platform—code, but also on the good description about what it does and how you can use the building blocks.

This book covers the most common tasks that are required during the data preparation and visualization phase of data analysis using KNIME. Because of the size constraints—and to bring the best price/value for those who are already familiar with or not interested in modeling—we have not covered the modeling and machine learning algorithms available for KNIME. If you are already familiar with these algorithms, you will easily get familiar with the options in KNIME, and these are quite obvious to use, so you lose almost nothing. If you have not found time yet to get acquainted with these concepts, we encourage you to first learn for what these procedures are good and when you should use them. There are some good books, courses, and training available—these are the ideal options for learning—but the Wikipedia articles can also give you a basic introduction specific to the algorithm you want to use.

What this book covers

Chapter 1, Installation and Using KNIME, introduces the user interface, the concepts used in the first three chapters, and how you can install and configure KNIME and its extensions.

Chapter 2, Data Preprocessing, covers the most common tasks, so that you can analyze your data, such as loading, transforming, and generating data; it also introduces the powerful regular expressions and some case studies.

Chapter 3, Data Exploration, describes how you can use KNIME to get an overview about your data, how you can visualize them in different forms, or even create publication quality figures.

Chapter 4, Reporting, introduces the KNIME reporting extension with the specific concepts, the user interface, and the basic blocks of reports.

What you need for this book

You only need a KNIME-compatible operating system, which is either a modern Linux, Mac OS X (10.6 or above), or Windows XP or above. The Java runtime is bundled with KNIME, and the first chapter describes how you can download and install KNIME. For this reason, you will need Internet connection too.

Who this book is for

This book is designed to give a good start to the data scientists who are not familiar with KNIME yet. Others, who are not familiar with programming, but need to load and transform their data in an intuitive way might also find this book useful.

Conventions

In this book, you will find a number of styles of text that distinguish among different kinds of information. Here are some examples of these styles, and an explanation of their meaning.

Code words in text are shown as follows: " In the first case, you have not much control about the details, for example, a `Pattern` object will be created for each call of the facade methods delegating to the `Pattern` class "

A block of code is set as follows:

```
// system imports
// Your custom imports:
import java.util.regex.*;
// system variables
// Your custom variables:
Pattern tuplePattern = Pattern.compile("\\((\\d+),\\s*(\\d+)\\)");
// expression start
```

```
// Enter your code here:
if (c_edge != null) {
  Matcher m = tuplePattern.matcher(c_edge);
  if (m.matches()) {
    out_edge = m.replaceFirst("($2, $1)");
  } else {
    out_edge = "NA";
  }
} else {
  out_edge = null;
}
// expression end
```

When we wish to draw your attention to a particular part of a code block, the relevant lines or items are set in bold:

```
// system imports
// Your custom imports:
import java.util.regex.*;
// system variables
// Your custom variables:
Pattern tuplePattern = Pattern.compile("\\((\\d+),\\s*(\\d+)\\)");
// expression start
// Enter your code here:
if (c_edge != null) {
  Matcher m = tuplePattern.matcher(c_edge);
  if (m.matches()) {
    out_edge = m.replaceFirst("($2, $1)");
  } else {
    out_edge = "NA";
  }
} else {
  out_edge = null;
}
// expression end
```

Any command-line input or output is written as follows:

```
$ tar -xvzf knime_2.8.0.linux.gtk.x86_64.tar.gz -C /path/to/extract
```

New terms and important words are shown in bold. Words that you see on the screen, in menus or dialog boxes for example, appear in the text like this: "Eclipse's main window is the **workbench**".

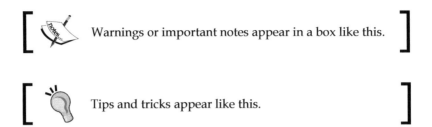

Warnings or important notes appear in a box like this.

Tips and tricks appear like this.

Reader feedback

Feedback from our readers is always welcome. Let us know what you think about this book—what you liked or may have disliked. Reader feedback is important for us to develop titles that you really get the most out of.

To send us general feedback, simply send an e-mail to feedback@packtpub.com, and mention the book title via the subject of your message.

If there is a topic in which you have expertise, and you are interested in either writing or contributing to a book, see our author guide on www.packtpub.com/authors.

Customer support

Now that you are the proud owner of a Packt book, we have a number of things to help you to get the most from your purchase.

Downloading the example code

You can download the example code files for all Packt books you have purchased from your account at http://www.packtpub.com. If you purchased this book elsewhere, you can visit http://www.packtpub.com/support and register to have the files e-mailed directly to you.

Errata

Although we have taken every care to ensure the accuracy of our content, mistakes do happen. If you find a mistake in one of our books—maybe a mistake in the text or the code—we would be grateful if you would report this to us. By doing so, you can save other readers from frustration and help us improve subsequent versions of this book. If you find any errata, please report them by visiting http://www.packtpub.com/submit-errata, selecting your book, clicking on the **errata submission form** link, and entering the details of your errata. Once your errata are verified, your submission will be accepted and the errata will be uploaded on our website, or added to any list of existing errata, under the Errata section of that title. Any existing errata can be viewed by selecting your title from http://www.packtpub.com/support.

Piracy

Piracy of copyright material on the Internet is an ongoing problem across all media. At Packt, we take the protection of our copyright and licenses very seriously. If you come across any illegal copies of our works, in any form, on the Internet, please provide us with the location address or website name immediately so that we can pursue a remedy.

Please contact us at copyright@packtpub.com with a link to the suspected pirated material.

We appreciate your help in protecting our authors, and our ability to bring you valuable content.

Questions

You can contact us at questions@packtpub.com if you are having a problem with any aspect of the book, and we will do our best to address it.

Installing and Using KNIME

1

In this chapter, we will go through the installation of KNIME, add some useful extensions, customize the settings, and find out how to use it for basic tasks. You will also be familiarized with the terminology of KNIME, so there's no misunderstanding in the later chapters.

As always, it is a good idea to read the manual of the software you get. You will find a short introduction on KNIME in the file, `quickstart.pdf`, present in the installation folder. The topics we will cover in the chapter are as follows:

- Installation of KNIME on different platforms
- Terms used in KNIME
- Introduction to the KNIME user interface

Few words about KNIME

KNIME is an open source (GNU GPL available at `http://www.gnu.org/licenses/gpl.html`) data analytics platform with a large set of building blocks and third-party tools. You can use it from loading your data to a final report or to predict new values using a previously found model.

KNIME is available in four flavors: Desktop/Professional, Team Space, Server, and Cluster Execution. Only the Desktop version is open source; with a Professional subscription, you will get support for it, and also support the future development of KNIME. We will cover only the open source version. There is also an SDK version for free, but it is intended for use by node developers. Most probably, you will not need it yet.

At the time of writing this book, KNIME Desktop 2.8.0 was the latest version available; all the information presented in this book is based on that version.

Installing KNIME

KNIME is supported by various operating systems on 32-bit and 64-bit x86 Intel-architecture-based platforms. These operating systems are: Windows (from XP to Windows 8 at the time of writing this book) and Linux (most modern Linux operating systems work well with KNIME, Mac OS X (10.6 and above); you can check the list of supported platforms for details at: http://www.eclipse.org/eclipse/development/readme_eclipse_3.7.1.html. It also supports Java 7 on Windows and Linux, so extensions requiring Java 7 can be used too. Unfortunately under Mac OS X, there were some problems with Java 7. So on Mac OS X, the recommended version is Java 6.

There are two ways to install KNIME: an easier way is to unpack the archive you can download from their site, and a bit more complicated way is to install KNIME to an existing Eclipse installation as a plugin. Both have use cases, but the general recommendation is to install it from an archive.

Installation using the archive

We assume you are using the open source version of KNIME, which can be downloaded from the following address (always download the latest version):

http://www.knime.org/knime-desktop-sdk-download

It is not necessary to subscribe to the newsletters, but if you have not done it yet, it might be worth doing it. Some of the newsletters also contain tips for KNIME usage. This is quite infrequent, usually one per month.

The supported operating system versions are 32-bit and 64-bit for Linux and Windows, and 64-bit for Mac OS X.

KNIME for Windows

KNIME is available in an executable file for Windows (in a 7-zip compressed format). You can execute it as a regular user (unless your network administrator blacklists running executable files that are downloaded from the Internet); just double-click on it and in the window that appears, select the destination folder.

> On an older version of Windows (7 and older), there is a limitation to the path length; it cannot be longer than 260 characters. KNIME and some extensions can get close to this limit, so it is recommended to install it to a short path. Installing it to Program Files is not recommended.

You do not have to specify the folder name (such as knime), as a folder with the name `knime_KNIME version` (in our case `knime_2.8.0`) will be created at the destination address, and it will contain the whole installation. You can have multiple versions installed.

You can start KNIME GUI with the `knime.exe` executable file from that folder. You can create a shortcut of it on your desktop using the right-click menu by navigating to **Send to | Desktop (create shortcut)**. On its first start, KNIME might ask for permissions to connect to the Internet. This may require administrator rights, but it is usually a good idea to change the firewall settings to let KNIME through.

KNIME for Linux

This file is just a simple `tar.gz` archive. You can unzip it using a command similar to the one shown as follows:

```
$ tar -xvzf knime_2.8.0.linux.gtk.x86_64.tar.gz -C /path/to/extract
```

Alternatively, you can use your favorite archive-handling tool to achieve similar results. The executable you need is named `knime`. Your window manager's manual might help you create application launchers for this executable if you prefer to have one.

KNIME for Mac OS X

You should drag the `dmg` file to the **Applications** place, and if you have Java installed, it should just work. The executable to start is called `knime.app` from the command line, `knime.app/Contents/MacOS/knime`.

Troubleshooting

If you have problems installing KNIME, maybe others also had similar problems; please check the FAQ page of KNIME at `http://tech.knime.org/faq` first. If it does not solve your problem, you should search the forum at `http://tech.knime.org/forum`; if even that fails to help, ask the experts there.

KNIME terminologies

It is important to share your thoughts and problems using the same terms. This makes it easier to reach your goal, and others will appreciate if it is easy to understand. This section will introduce the main concepts of KNIME.

Organizing your work

In KNIME, you store your files in a **workspace**. When KNIME starts, you can specify which workspace you want to use. The workspaces are not just for files; they also contain settings and logs. It might be a good idea to set up an empty workspace, and instead of customizing a new one each time, you start a new project; you just copy (extract) it to the place you want to use, and open it with KNIME (or switch to it).

The workspace can contain **workflow group**s (sometimes referred to as **workflow set**) or **workflow**s. The groups are like folders in a filesystem that can help organize your workflows. Workflows might be your *programs* and *processes* that describe the steps which should be applied to load, analyze, visualize, or transform the data you have, something like an execution plan. Workflows contain the executable parts, which can be edited using the **workflow editor**, which in turn is similar to a canvas. Both the groups and the workflows might have metadata associated with them, such as the creation date, author, or comments (even the workspace can contain such information).

Workflows might contain *nodes*, *meta nodes*, *connections*, *workflow variables* (or just *flow variables*), *workflow credentials*, and *annotations* besides the previously introduced metadata.

Workflow credentials is the place where you can store your *login name* and *password* for different connections. These are kept safe, but you can access them easily.

 It is safe to share a workflow if you use only the workflow credentials for sensitive information (although the user name will be saved).

Nodes

Each node has a type, which identifies the algorithm associated with the node. You can think of the type as a template; it specifies how to execute for different inputs and parameters, and what should be the result. The nodes are similar to functions (or operators) in programs.

The node types are organized according to the following general types, which specify the color and the shape of the node for easier understanding of workflows. The general types are shown in the following image:

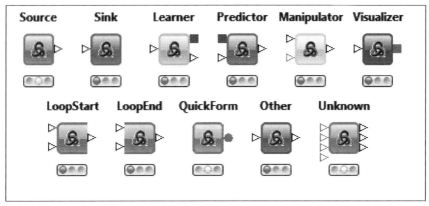

Example representation of different general types of nodes

The nodes are organized in categories; this way, it is easier to find them.

Each node has a *node documentation* that describes what can be achieved using that type of node, possibly use cases or tips. It also contains information about *parameters* and possible *input ports* and *output ports*. (Sometimes the last two are called *inports* and *outports*, or even *in-ports* and *out-ports*.)

Parameters are usually single values (for example, *filename, column name, text, number, date*, and so on) associated with an identifier; although, having an array of texts is also possible. These are the settings that influence the execution of a node. There are other things that can modify the results, such as workflow variables or any other state observable from KNIME.

Node lifecycle

Nodes can have any of the following states:

- Misconfigured (also called IDLE)
- Configured
- Queued for execution
- Running
- Executed

There are possible warnings in most of the states, which might be important; you can read them by moving the mouse pointer over the triangle sign.

Meta nodes

Meta nodes look like normal nodes at first sight, although they contain other nodes (or meta nodes) inside them. The associated context of the node might give options for special execution. Usually they help to keep your workflow organized and less scary at first sight.

A user-defined meta node

Ports

The ports are where data in some form flows through from one node to another. The most common port type is the **data table**. These are represented by white triangles. The input ports (where data is expected to get into) are on the left-hand side of the nodes, but the output ports (where the created data comes out) are on the right-hand side of the nodes. You cannot mix and match the different kinds of ports. It is also not allowed to connect a node's output to its input or create circles in the graph of nodes; you have to create a loop if you want to achieve something similar to that.

 Currently, all ports in the standard KNIME distribution are presenting the results only when they are ready; although the infrastructure already allows other strategies, such as streaming, where you can view partial results too.

The ports might contain information about the data even if their nodes are not yet executed.

Data tables

These are the most common form of port types. It is similar to an Excel sheet or a data table in the database. Sometimes these are named example set or data frame.

Each data table has a *name*, a *structure* (or schema, a table specification), and possibly *properties*. The structure describes the data present in the table by storing some properties about the *columns*. In other contexts, columns may be called attributes, variables, or features.

A column can only contain data of a single type (but the types form a hierarchy from the top and can be of any type). Each column has a *type*, a *name*, and a *position* within the table. Besides these, they might also contain further information, for example, statistics about the contained values or color/shape information for visual representation. There is always something in the data tables that looks like a column, even if it is not really a column. This is where the identifiers for the *rows* are held, that is, the *row keys*.

There can be multiple rows in the table, just like in most of the other data handling software (similar to observations or records). The row keys are unique (textual) identifiers within the table. They have multiple roles besides that; for example, usually row keys are the labels when showing the data, so always try to find user-friendly identifiers for the rows.

At the intersection of rows and columns are the (data) *cells*, similar to the data found in Excel sheets or in database tables (whereas in other contexts, it might refer to the data similar to values or fields). There is a special cell that represents the *missing values*.

The missing value is usually represented as a question mark (?).

If you have to represent more information about the missing data, you should consider adding a new column for each column, where this requirement is present, and add that information; however, in the original column, you just declare it as missing.

There are multiple cell types in KNIME, and the following table contains the most important ones:

Cell type	Symbol	Remarks
Int cell	I	This represents integral numbers in the range from -2^{31} to $2^{31}-1$ (approximately 2E9).
Long cell	L	This represents larger integral numbers, and their range is from -2^{63} to $2^{63}-1$ (approximately 9E18).
Double cell	D	This represents real numbers with double (64 bit) floating point precision.
String cell	S	This represents unstructured textual information.

Cell type	Symbol	Remarks
Date and time cell	calendar & clock	With these cells, you can store either date or time.
Boolean cell	B	This represents logical values from the Boolean algebra (true or false); note that you cannot exclude the missing value.
Xml cell	XML	This cell is ideal for structured data.
Set cell	{...}	This cell can contain multiple cells (so a collection cell type) of the same type (no duplication or order of values are preserved).
List cell	{...}	This is also a collection cell type, but this keeps the order and does not filter out the duplicates.
Unknown type cell	?	When you have different type of cells in a column (or in a collection cell), this is the generic cell type used.

There are other cell types, for example, the ones for chemical data structures (SMILES, CDK, and so on), for images (SVG cell, PNG cell, and so on), or for documents. This is extensible, so the other extension can define custom data cell types.

 Note that any data cell type can contain the missing value.

Port view

The port view allows you to get information about the content of the port. Complete content is available only after the node is executed, but usually some information is available even before that. This is very handy when you are constructing the workflow. You can check the structure of the data even if you will usually use *node view* in the later stages of data exploration during workflow construction.

Flow variables

Workflows can contain flow variables, which can act as a loop counter, a column name, or even an expression for a node parameter. These are not constants, but you can introduce them to the workspace level as well.

This is a powerful feature; once you master it, you can create workflows you thought were impossible to create using KNIME. A typical use case for them is to assign roles to different columns (by assigning the column names to the role name as a flow variable) and use this information for node configurations. If your workflow has some important parameters that should be adjusted or set before each execution (for example a file name), this is an ideal option to provide these to the user; use the flow variables instead of a preset value that is hard to find. As the automatic generation of figures gets more support, the flow variables will find use there too.

Iterating a range of values or files in a folder should also be done using flow variables.

Node views

Nodes can also have *node views* associated with them. These help to visualize your data or a model, show the node's internal state, or select a subset of the data using the **HiLite** feature. An important feature exists that a node's views can be opened multiple times. This allows us to compare different options of visualization without taking screenshots or having to remember what was it like, and how you reached that state. You can export these views to image files.

HiLite

The HiLite feature of KNIME is quite unique. Its purpose is to help identify a group of data that is important or interesting for some reason. This is related to the node views, as this selection is only visible in nodes with node views (for example, it is not available in port views). Support for data *high lighting* is optional, because not all views support this feature.

The HiLite selection data is based on row keys, and this information can be lost when the row keys change. For this reason, some of the nonview nodes also have an option to keep this information propagated to the adjacent nodes. On the other hand, when the row keys remain the same, the marks in different views point to the same data rows.

It is very important that the HiLite selection is only visible in a well-connected subgraph of workflow. It can also be available for non-executed nodes (for example, the *HiLite Collector node*).

 The HiLite information is *not* saved in the workflow, so you should use the *HiLite filter node* once you are satisfied with your selection to save that state, and you can reset that HiLite later.

Eclipse concepts

Because KNIME is based on the Eclipse platform (http://eclipse.org), it inherits some of its features too. One of them is the *workspace model* with projects (workflows in case of KNIME), and another important one is *modularity*. You can extend KNIME's functionality using plugins and features; sometimes these are named KNIME **extensions**. The extensions are distributed through *update sites*, which allow you to install updates or install new software from a local folder, a zip file, or an Internet location.

The help system, the update mechanism (with proxy settings), or the file search feature are also provided by Eclipse. Eclipse's main window is the **workbench**. The most typical features are the **perspectives** and the **views**. Perspectives are about how the parts of the UI are arranged, while these independently configurable parts are the views. These views have nothing to do with node views or port views. The Eclipse/KNIME views can be detached, closed, moved around, minimized, or maximized within the window. Usually each view can have at most one instance visible (the **Console** view is an exception). KNIME does not support alternative perspectives (arrangements of views), so it is not important for you; however, you can still reset it to its original state.

It might be important to know that Eclipse keeps the contents of files and folders in a special form. If you generate files, you should refresh the content to load it from the filesystem. You can do this from the context menu, but it can also be automated if you prefer that option.

Preferences

The preferences are associated with the workspace you use. This is where most of the Eclipse and KNIME settings are to be specified. The node parameters are stored in the workflows (which are also within the workspace), and these parameters are not considered to be preferences.

Logging

KNIME has something to tell you about almost every action. Usually, you do not care to read these logs, you do not need to do so. For this reason, KNIME dispatches these messages using different channels. There is a file in the workplace that collects all the messages by default with considerable details. There is even a KNIME/Eclipse view named **Console**, which contains only the most important details initially.

User interface

So far, you got familiar with the concepts of KNIME and also installed it. Let's run it!

Getting started

When you start the program, the first dialog asks for the location of the workspace you want to use. If the location does not exist, it will be created.

After this, a splash screen will inform you about the progress of the start, and bring you to the welcome screen.

In the background, your firewall might notify you that this program wants to connect to other computers. This is normal; it loads tips from the Internet and tests whether other services (for example, the public repository of KNIME workflows) are available or not. You can allow this if you have permission to do so, but unless you want to connect to other servers, you do not have to give that permission.

The welcome screen shows two main options: one for initializing the workbench for first use, and the other is to install new extensions.

Before we select either of them, we will introduce the most important preferences, because configuring before the first use is always useful.

Setting preferences

Navigate to the **Preferences...** menu item under **File | Preferences...** to gain access to the preferences dialog. In the **General** section, you will see an option to enable **Show heap status**. It is useful, because it can help you optimize the memory settings for KNIME. I suggest you to turn it on. It will be visible in the lower-right corner of the status bar.

KNIME

You can set some KNIME-related options in the preferences of the **KNIME** category.

The **KNIME GUI** subcategory contains confirmation, **Console** logging, workflow editor grid options, and some text-related options.

If you want to connect to databases, you should find a driver for your database, and register it by navigating to **KNIME | Database Driver**. There, you can add the archive file, and later, you will be able to use them in database connections.

Database drivers

You can find JDBC database drivers on your database provider's homepage, but you can also try the JDBC database: http://www.databasedrivers.com/jdbc/

With **Preferred Renderers** you can set the default renderers for the columns. This options is especially useful if you are working with chemical structures.

The main **KNIME** preference page contains the file logging detail settings, the parallelism option, and the path to the temporary files.

Other preferences

To set up the proxy, you should navigate to **General | Network Connections**.

In the **General | Keys** page, you can redefine the key bindings for KNIME commands. So, you can use the shortcuts with which you are familiar or comfortable on your keyboard.

General | Web Browser and the **Help** pages are especially useful when you have problems displaying help, or you want to browse local help in your browser.

You can also set some update sites by navigating to **Install/Update | Available Software Sites**, but usually that is also done by navigating to **Help | Install New Software...**.

You can uninstall extensions by navigating to **Help | About KNIME** behind the **Installation Details** button's dialog. The **Installed Software** tab contains the extensions; you can uninstall them with a button.

Installing extensions

For installing extensions you need some update sites. You already have the default KNIME options, which contain some useful extensions. There are community nodes that also add helpful functionality to KNIME. The stable update site is http://tech.knime.org/update/community-contributions/2.8, while nightly builds are available at http://tech.knime.org/update/community-contributions/nightly.

To add update sites, navigate to **Help | Install New Software...**. Once you have selected an update site, it will download its summary so you can select which extensions (features) you want to install. These features have short descriptions, so you can have an idea what functionality it will offer after installation. Once you have selected what you want to install from the update site, you should click **Next**.

The wizard's next page gives some details and summaries about the selected features.

On the next page, you can check the licenses and accept them if you are OK with them. After clicking **Finish**, the installation starts. During the installation, you might be asked to check whether you really want to install extensions with unsigned content, or you want to accept a signing key. Once it is ready, you will be asked to restart your workbench. After restarting it, you can use the features that were installed; however, sometimes there are some preferences to be set before using them.

Workbench

So far, we have set up the work environment and installed some extensions. Now let's select the large button named **Open KNIME Workbench**.

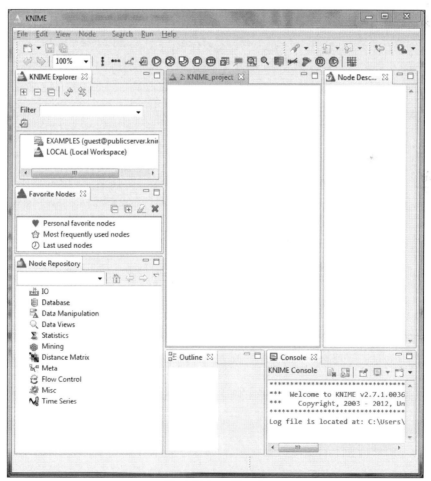

The initial workbench

The menu bar is similar to any other menu bar, just like the toolbars and the status bar. We will cover the menu bar and the toolbar in detail.

The **KNIME Explorer** view can be used to handle your workflows, workflow groups, or connect to KNIME servers. The **Favorite Nodes** view contains the favorite, last used, and most used nodes as a shortcut. You can specify the maximum number of items that should be there.

> You should play with the view controls a bit more and get familiar with their usage.

Node Repository is one of the most important views. It contains nodes organized in categories. The search box is really helpful when it comes to the workflow design, and if you remember a part of the name but not its category. You will use this feature quite often.

The **Outline** view gives an overview on what is in the current editor window; it can also help navigating if the window is too large.

> It is considered bad practice to have a single, huge workflow for your task. Using meta nodes, you can have more compact parts in every level.

The **Console** view contains messages—initially only the important ones.

The **Node Description** tab provides you with help information for the selected node. Information on how you should use it, what are the parameters, what should be its input, what is its output, and what kind of views are available are answered in that tab. When you select a category in the **Node Repository** view, the contents of the category will be displayed.

And finally, the central area of the window is for the *workflow editor*. A workflow named **KNIME_project** was created. Now, you can start working on it. Try adding the **File Reader** node from the **IO | Read** category in **Node Repository**. Drag it from the repository to the workflow or just double-click it in the repository, move it around, add another, delete it using the context menu, and that would be a good start.

The **Undo** (*Ctrl + Z*) and **Redo** (*Ctrl + Y*) commands from the **Edit** or the context menu (or from the toolbar: curved left and right arrows) can help you go back to the previous editing state.

Workflow handling

To create a workflow group, open the context menu of the **LOCAL (Local Workspace)** item in the **KNIME Explorer** view and select **New Workflow Group...** from the menu. Specify the name of the workflow group and where it should be created (once you have more groups, you can create groups inside those too). Creating a workflow can also be done using the **New Workflow...** command. These commands are also available from the **File | New...** (*Ctrl + N*) dialog.

> The key bindings are not always easy to remember because there are many of them; for more information and help about them, navigate to the **Help | Key Assist...** menu item or use *Ctrl + Shift + L.*

To load a workflow, first you have to make it available locally. There are many options to do that. You can import it to the workspace using the **File | Import KNIME workflow...** dialog (also available from the context menu).

> There is a file named `ExampleFlow.zip` in the installation folder; you can use that.

> The **Example Flow** workflow loads the iris dataset (do not reset that node), colors the rows according to their class label, and visualizes the data in three different ways.

Another option is to download a workflow from the KNIME Server. Fortunately, the public KNIME Server is available for guests too. First you have to log in using the context menu. Select the only available option, **Login**. Once the catalog has been loaded, you can browse it similar to what you can do with the local workspace. But you cannot open the workflow from there. You have to select the one you want to import and copy it (in the context menu, use **Copy** or press *Ctrl + C*). Once you have the right place in the local workspace, insert the workflow (in the context menu use **Paste**, or press *Ctrl + V*).

The metadata information can be handy if you want to know when it was created, who the author is, or what did someone comment. The comment information is especially handy if you want to choose the workflow you want to download. To get (or set for local workflows) this information, the context menu's **Show Meta Information** (or **Edit Meta Information...**) command should be used.

Describe your dependencies

If you mention the prerequisites to your workflow, it will help the next user (who may be the future you) to set up things properly.

In loaded workflows, sometimes there are yellow notes about the structure of the workflow to grab your attention for customization options, and others. You can create your own notes from the context menu of the workflow editor using the **New Workflow Annotation** menu item. You can close the workflow by closing its editor.

The context menu gives options to **Rename...** (*F2*) (only available for closed workflows), **Delete...** (*Delete*), **Copy** (*Ctrl + C*), **Paste** (*Ctrl + V*), or **Cut** (*Ctrl + X*)—or just move using dragging—workflows or workflow groups.

The quickstart.pdf file describes how you can export workflows to share them with other users. The web guide for this is available at:
http://tech.knime.org/workbench#export

Node controls

Once you have nodes in the editor, you want to configure it. To do that, you should double-click it, select it from the context menu or the **Node** menu using the **Configure...** command, or use the toolbar's checklist icon (also accessible by pressing *F6*). This opens a configuration dialog (**Line Reader** node), as shown in the following screenshot:

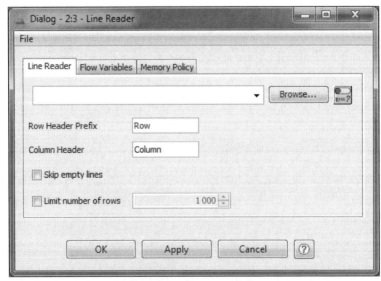

Example configuration dialog

This way you can set the parameters of the node. There can be various controls, usually with helpful tooltips; you can open them in a side window, and add the node description too. You might wonder what should that **v=?** button do. It opens up the variable settings. For example, you can use the filename in subsequent nodes as a flow variable, or substitute it with a flow variable, if that is what you need.

The configurations are organized in tabs. The last two tabs are present in all the configuration dialogs. The **Flow Variables** tab allows you to assign flow variables to the parameters as values, as shown in the following screenshot:

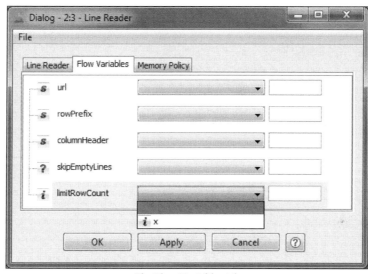

The Flow Variables tab

The **Memory Policy** tab is seldom needed; you can specify how the data should be handled within KNIME during execution of the node, as shown in the following screenshot:

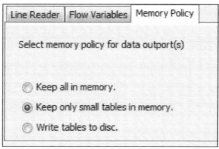

The Memory Policy tab

It really helps to identify the nodes or their purpose if you give them meaningful names. To change the name, click on a previously selected node or press *F2*. If you want more detailed information, you might consider adding a workflow annotation around it. Alternatively, you might want to add a node description to it by navigating to the context menu item **Edit Node Description...**, or the **Node** menu **Edit Node Name and Description...** (*Alt + F2*), or by clicking the toolbar's yellow speech balloon. This information will be the tooltip of the node.

If you find the names distracting or if they are the default name, you can hide or enable them by navigating to **Node | Hide Node Names**, by pressing *Ctrl + Alt + Q* or the stroked through text on the toolbar.

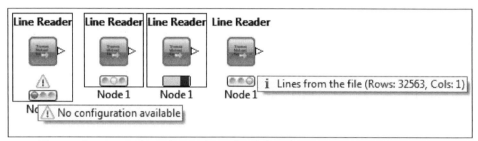

The way from not configured to configured, and then the executing and executed states.

We want to execute the node to get the results. To achieve this, select the context menu or the **Node** menu, and select **Execute** (*F7*). On the toolbar, this is the *play* button (a white triangle on green circle). You can also schedule execution to show the first view after that (*Shift + F10*). You can change your mind and try to stop the execution before it is finished. For this purpose, navigate to **Node | Cancel Execution** (*F9*) of the selected nodes, or navigate to **Node | Cancel All Execution** (*Shift + F9*).

There might be warnings or errors even after the execution; you will be notified about those.

If the execution finishes successfully, you can check the ports by selecting one of them from the context menu; alternatively, if you want to check the first output port, navigate to **Node | Open First Out-Port View** (*Shift + F6*, a magnifier over a table on the toolbar). Checking views is a good idea too (it can be selected from the context menu or via **Node | Open First View**, *F10*, a magnifier on the toolbar). The node views also have some common parts: the **File** and the **HiLite** menus.

If you make changes to the configuration, your node will be reset to the configured state; it can also be achieved using **Node** or the context menu's **Reset** (*F8*) command (or the toolbar's x-table button). The reset will not delete the previously set parameters.

To connect a node's output port to another node's input port, just drag the output port to the input port; when the mouse button is released they will be connected (assuming the ports are compatible and would not create cycle in the graph of nodes). From one output port, you can connect to as many input nodes as you want (to same nodes too), but the input ports can only handle one port at the most.

There are arrangement commands available on the toolbar (horizontal, vertical, and auto layout), and you can also configure the node snapping grid properties by navigating to **Node | Grid Settings...** (*Ctrl + Alt + Shift + X*) from the toolbar—a grid.

HiLite

As we mentioned previously, HiLite is a view-related feature of KNIME, which allows selecting certain set of rows and making it visible across different rows. The Example Flow is a good start to get familiar with this concept and see it in action. As you can see, there are four visual type nodes available, the **Color Manager**, **Scatter Plot**, **Parallel Coordinates**, and **Interactive table**. Please open a view for the last three nodes, and also execute them in the same order.

The interactive table node shows data with different colors for different flowers. Select the first **Iris-versicolor** row, **51**. Now from the **HiLite** menu, select **HiLite selected** (also available from the context menu in this view). As you can see, a point and a path has already been highlighted on the other two views—those representing the row **51**. If you try, you can highlight another row from the **Interactive table** view; you can select some dots from the scatter plot or paths from the parallel coordinates. Highlighting them can be done similar to what you did in the first view. You also have the option to selectively unhighlight (**UnHiLite Selected**) or unhighlight all (**Clear HiLite**). You can also hide or keep only the highlighted rows (in the view, the port content will not be changed) using the **HiLite | Filter** menu items.

To store the HiLite information, you should add **HiLite Filter** (for example, add it to the **Color Manager** node), execute them, and save the workflow. With the **Interactive HiLite Collector** node, you can add custom information to the currently highlighted rows, so that later you can identify multiple subsets (if you check the **New Column** box before clicking on **Apply**). Do not forget to execute the node, and later save the workflow once you are satisfied with your selection.

Variable flows

When you bring your mouse cursor to the left and upper-right corner of the nodes (a bit outside of it), you will get a different tooltip—**Variable Inport** and **Variable Outport (Variables Connection)** respectively. Something useful is hidden there. Select a node, and from the context menu, select **Show Flow Variable Ports**. This way two circles will appear filled with the color red. You can connect them to the other node's input/output flow ports. These connections are red. This way you can make sure the proper set of variables will be available at the right time (circular dependencies are not allowed this way). The loops also use the workflow variables, and there are multiple nodes to create these or change them. You seldom need these connections as flow variables are propagated through normal connections.

You can also specify workflow variables from the context menu of the workflow (**Workflow Variables...**), or by using the QuickForm nodes.

Meta nodes

We mentioned that the meta nodes are useful for encapsulating the parts of the workflow and to hide the distracting details. The `quickstart.pdf` file gives a nice introduction to meta nodes; you can find the content on the web too at the link `http://tech.knime.org/metanodes`.

An unmentioned option to create new meta nodes is by selecting a closed subset of non-executed nodes or meta nodes and invoking the **Collapse into Meta Node** action from the context menu. The opposite process (bringing the contents of the meta node to the current level) is also possible with the **Expand Meta Node** context menu item.

Opening a meta node is possible by double-clicking on it or selecting the **Open Meta Node** context menu item. Both ways, another workflow editor tab will appear, where you can continue the workflow design.

Workflow lifecycle

Once you have a workflow, you might want to save the changes you made and the computed data and models. That is really easy; navigate to **File | Save** (*Ctrl + S*) or use the toolbar's disc icon.

 You cannot save workflows with executing nodes, so you have to save them before or later, else you have to stop the execution.

Sometimes you want to execute the whole workflow. To do that, you can use the toolbar's **Execute all executable nodes** button (a fast forward icon with a green circle background, *Shift + F8*) or the **Node | Execute All** menu item.

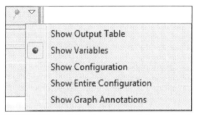

Batch processing

To process workflows from the command line (or from other program), the KNIME FAQ gives a good description at the following link: `http://tech.knime.org/faq#q12`

If there are multiple entry points to your workflow, it can be boring to reset all those nodes one by one, but the **Reset** command from the context menu of **KNIME Explorer** will reset all the nodes in the selected workflow.

Other views

The **Server Workflow Projects** view shows only the workflows (and groups) available on servers, but the **Workflow Projects** view shows only the local ones. If you do not need server workflows, this might be a better choice than the **KNIME Explorer** view, as this is more compact.

KNIME Node Monitor (View | Other... | KNIME Views) view gives you information about the selected item's state and other parameters. I think you will find this useful, especially if you explore the dropdown menu from the white triangle:

	Show Output Table
●	Show Variables
	Show Configuration
	Show Entire Configuration
	Show Graph Annotations

KNIME Node Monitor's possible contents

Summary

In this chapter, we have installed KNIME, set it up for its first usage, configured it, and installed a few extensions. We also went through the most important concepts you will use. We started using the workflow editor and executed our first workflow. Now it is time for you to check some of the example workflows from the KNIME public server and try to execute and modify them.

2
Data Preprocessing

Data preprocessing usually takes a lot of time to set up, because you have to take care of lot of different formats or sources. In this chapter, we will introduce the basic options to not only read and generate data but also to reshape them. Changing values is also a common task, and we will cover that too.

It is a good practice to keep checking certain constraints especially if you have volatile input sources. This is also important in KNIME. Finally, we will go through an example of workflow from import to preprocessing. In this chapter, we will cover the following topics:

- Data import
    - From database
    - From files
    - From web services

- Regular expressions
- Transforming tables
- Transforming values
- Generating data
- Constraints
- Case studies

Importing data

Your data can be from multiple sources, such as databases, Internet/intranet, or files. This section will give a short introduction to the various options.

Importing data from a database

In this section, we will use the Java DB (http://www.oracle.com/technetwork/java/javadb/index.html) to create a local database because it is supported by Oracle, bundled with JDKs, cross-platform, and easy to set up. The database we use is described on eclipse's **BIRT Sample Database** page (http://www.eclipse.org/birt/phoenix/db/#schema).

Starting Java DB

Once you have Java DB installed (unzipped the binary distribution from Derby (http://db.apache.org/derby/derby_downloads.html) or located your JDK), you should also download the BirtSample.jar file from this book's website (originally from http://mirror-fpt-telecom.fpt.net/eclipse/birt/update-site/3.7-interim/plugins/org.eclipse.birt.report.data.oda.sampledb_3.7.2.v20120213.jar.pack.gz). Unzip the content to the database server's install folder.

You should start a terminal from the database server's home folder, using the following command:

```
bin/startNetworkServer
```

 You can stop it with the bin/stopNetworkServer command.

Locate the database server's lib/derbyclicnt.jar file. You should install this driver as described in the previous chapter (**File | Preferences | KNIME | Database Driver**).

You can import the DatabaseConnection.zip file, downloaded from this book's website, as a KNIME workflow. This time, we were not using workflow credentials as it would always be asked for on load, and it might be hard to remember the ClassicModels password.

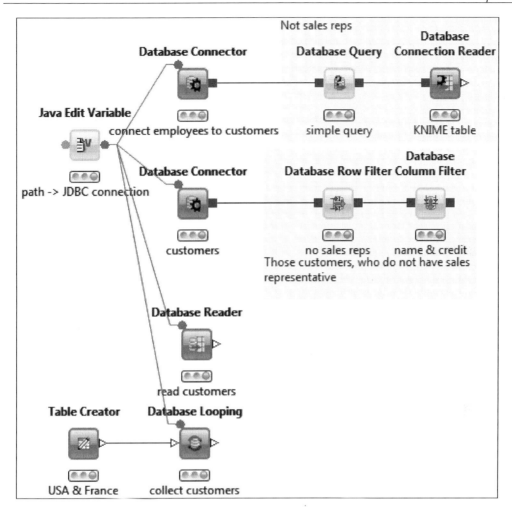

The previous screenshot reads different tables and filter some of the results. The **Java Edit Variable** node provides the JDBC connection string as a flow variable.

There is a workflow variable named database location (default value: BirtSample), in case you want to specify an absolute path to the database you want to use. The **Java Edit Variable** node appends this path to the default local database connection, so you can use the Derby JDBC connection variable in the subsequent nodes. You should start with executing this node to configure the other nodes.

The **Database Connector** node can connect to the database and give a stub for further processing (you can inspect it using the port viewer, though, once you execute).

The **Database Query** can be used to express complex conditions in the table. Please be careful. You should name the #table#, like we did in the following query:

```
SELECT * FROM #table# customerTable where customernumber < 300 or
customernumber is null
```

Downloading the example code

You can download the example code files for all Packt books you have purchased from your account at http://www.packtpub.com. If you purchased this book elsewhere, you can visit http://www.packtpub.com/support and register to have the files e-mailed directly to you.

If you have simpler (single column) conditions, you can also use the **Database Row Filter** node. Removal of a few columns (projection) can be performed with the **Database Column Filter** node.

If you want to process or visualize the data in KNIME, you have to convert the database connection port type to regular data tables using the **Database Connection Reader** node. If you do not need post-processing of the database tables, you can simply specify the connection and the query with the **Database Reader** node.

An interesting option to read data is by using the **Database Looping** node. It can read the values from one of the input table's columns and select only the values that match a subset of the column for one of the database columns' values.

Exercise

Check what happens if you uncheck the **Aggregate by row** option or increase the **No of Values per Query** parameter.

You also have the option to modify the database, such as deleting rows, updating certain rows, creating tables, and appending records. For details, check the **Database Delete**, **Database Update**, and **Database Writer** nodes. While replacing/creating a table for an existing database, the connection can be performed using the **Database Connection Writer** node.

Importing data from tabular files

This time, for example, we will load a simple comma-separated file. For this purpose, you can use the **File Reader** node and the following link:

```
http://archive.ics.uci.edu/ml/machine-learning-databases/iris/iris.
data
```

KNIME will automatically set the parameters, although you have to specify the column names (the `http://archive.ics.uci.edu/ml/machine-learning-databases/iris/iris.names` file gives a description of the dataset).

In the configuration dialog, you can refine the columns in the preview area by clicking on its header.

Naturally, you can open the local files too, if you specify the URL using the **Browse...** button.

If you have the data in the Excel format, you might need the **KNIME XLS Support** extension from the standard KNIME update site. This way, you will be able to read (with the **XLS Reader** node) and also write the `xls` files (with the **XLS Writer** node).

 The extension can also read the `xlsx` files, but cannot write them.

Just like the **File Reader** node, **XLS Reader** can load the files from the Internet too. (If you have the data in the `ods` format, you have to convert/export it to either the `xls(x)` or the `csv` file to be able to load from KNIME.)

The **CSV Reader** node is less important if you prefer to use the KNIME Desktop product; however, with the batch mode, you might find this node useful (less options for configuration, but it can provide the file name as a flow variable).

 Try dragging a file which can be imported on the editor area.

Attribute-Relation File Format (ARFF) is also tabular (`http://weka.wikispaces.com/ARFF`). You can read them with the **ARFF Reader** node. Exporting to ARFF can be done with **ARFF Writer**.

Importing data from web services

For **Web Services Description Language (WSDL)** web services, you can use the **KNIME Webservice Client** standard extension. It provides the **Generic Webservice Client** node.

This node gives many advanced features to access WSDL services, but you should test it to see whether or not it is compatible with your service interface before implementing a new one. It is based on Apache CXF (http://cxf.apache.org/), so any limitation of that project is a limitation of this node too.

Unfortunately, not much WSDL web services are available for free without registration, but you can try it out at http://www.webservicex.com/globalweather.asmx?wsdl. Naturally, if you are registered for another service, or you have an own in the intranet, you can give it a try.

REST services

Nowadays, the **REST (Representational State Transfer)** services has gathered momentum, so it is always nice if you can use it too. In this regard, I would recommend the next section where we introduce the **XML Reader** node. You can use the KREST (http://tech.knime.org/book/krest-rest-nodes-for-knime) nodes to handle the JSON or XML REST queries.

Importing XML files

You need the **KNIME XML-Processing** extension from the standard KNIME update site. The **XML Reader** node can parse either local or external files, which you can further analyze or transform.

Importing models

Once you have a model, you might want to save it (**Model Writer** or **PMML Writer**) to use it later in other workflows. In those workflows, you can use the **Model Reader** or **PMML Reader** nodes to bring these models to the new workflow.

Other formats

Some extensions also provide reader nodes to certain data types. The standard KNIME update site contains multiple chemical extensions supporting different formats of chemical compounds.

The **KNIME Labs Update Site** extensions support text processing, graphs, and logfile analyzing, and they contain readers for these tasks.

Public data sources

Most probably you are already familiar with the available data sources for your area of research/work, although a short list of generic data collections might interest you in order to improve the results of your data analysis.

Here are some of them:

- Open data (http://en.wikipedia.org/wiki/Open_data) members, such as **DATA.GOV** (http://www.data.gov/) and **European Union Open Data Portal** (http://open-data.europa.eu/)
- **Freebase** (http://www.freebase.com/)
- **WIKIDATA** (http://www.wikidata.org/wiki/Wikidata:Main_Page)
- **DBpedia** (http://dbpedia.org/)
- **YAGO2** (http://www.mpi-inf.mpg.de/yago-naga/yago/)
- **Windows Azure Marketplace** (http://datamarket.azure.com/)

This was just a short list; you can find many more of these, and the list of data sources for specific areas would be even longer.

Regular expressions

Regular expressions are excellent for simpler parsing tasks, replaces, or splits. We will give a short introduction on them and show some examples. These will allow you to get better idea. At the end of this section, we will suggest further reading.

Basic syntax

Usually, when you write a text as a pattern, this means that the text will be matched; for example, `apple or pear` will match the highlighted parts from the following sentence: "`Apple stores do not sell` **`apple or pear`**."

These are case sensitive by default, so if the pattern were to be simply `apple`, this will not match the first word of the sentence or the company name.

There are special characters that need to be escaped when you want to match them: `.`, `[`, `]`, `(`, `)`, `{`, `}`, `-`, `^`, `$`, `\` (Well, some of these only in certain positions). To escape them, you should prefix them with `\`, which will result in the following patterns: `\.`, `\[`, `\]`, `\(`, `\)`, `\{`, `\}`, `\-`, `\^`, `\$`, `\\`.

When you do not want an exact match of characters, you can use the [characters] brackets around the possible options, such as [abc], which will match either **a**, **b**, or **c** but not bc (not a single character) or d (not among the options). You can specify the range of characters using the character within brackets, such as [a-z], which will match any lower case English alphabet characters. You can have multiple ranges and values within brackets, such as [a-zA-Z,], which will match either a lowercase or an uppercase character or a comma (equivalent to [[a-z][A-Z][,]] but not to [a-z] [A-Z][,] because the latter would match three characters, not one).

To negate a certain character class, you can use the ^ character within brackets; for example, the [^0-9] pattern will match a single character except the digits (or the line separators).

It might be tedious and error prone to specify always certain groups of characters, so there are special sets/classes predefined. Here is a non-exhaustive list of the most important ones:

- \d: It identifies the decimal digits ([0-9])
- \s: It identifies the whitespace characters
- \n: It identifies a new line character (by default, only single lines are handled so new lines cannot be matched in that mode, but you can specify a multiline match too)
- \w: It identifies the English alphabet (identifier) characters and decimal digits ([a-zA-Z_0-9])

You can also use the groups within brackets to complement them; for example, [^\d\s] (a character that is neither a whitespace nor a digit).

These can be used when you know in advance how long you want to match the parts; although, usually this is not the case. You can specify a range for the number of times you want to match certain patterns using the {n,m} syntax, where *n* and *m* are nonnegative numbers; for example, [ab]{1,3} will match the following: a, aa, aaa, and bab but not baba or the empty string.

When you do not specify *m* in the previously mentioned syntax, it will be (right) unbounded the number of times it can appear. When you omit the comma sign too, the preceding pattern has to appear exactly *n* times to get a match.

There are shorter versions for {0,1} - **?**, {0,} - *****, {1,} - **+**.

When there is no suffix for these numeric or symbolic quantifiers, you are using the greedy match; if you append ?, it implies the reluctant; while if you append a + sign, it will be possessive. Here are some examples: [ab]+b, [ab]+?b, and [ab]++b. The details are important, and can be shown by example. We will highlight the matches for certain patterns and texts (we will separate the matches with | if there are multiple):

Text\ pattern	[ab]+b	[ab]+?b	[ab]++b	[ab]+?	[ab]++
abababbb	**abababbb**	ab|ab|ab|bb	abababbb	a|b|a|b|a|b|b|b	**abababbb**
ababa	**ababa**	ab|aba	ababa	a|b|a|b|a	**ababa**
abb	**abb**	**abb**	abb	a|b|b	**abb**

The last column is a whole text match for each example, also the first column's first and third patterns, but all other examples are just partial (or no) matches.

You might want to create more complex conditions, but you need grouping of certain patterns for them. There are capturing groups and non-capturing groups. The capturing groups can be referred to with their number (there is always an implicit capturing group for each match and the whole match; that is, the *0* group), but the non-capturing groups are not available for further reference or processing, although they can be very useful when you want to separate unwanted parts. The syntax for capturing groups is (subpattern) and for non-capturing groups is (?:subpattern).

When you want to refer back to previous groups, you should use the \n notation, where *n* is the index of the previous group (in the pattern, the start of the nth starting group parentheses).

There is also an option to create named groups using the (?<name>subpattern) syntax. (This feature is available since Java 7, so it will not work on Mac OS X until you can use KNIME with Java 7 or a later version.) Referring to named patterns can be done with the \k<name> syntax.

With these groups, you can express not just more kinds of quantification, but also alternatives using the | (or) construct, for example (ab)?((?:[cd]+)|(?:xzy)), which means that there is optionally a group of ab characters followed by some sequence of c or d characters or the text xzy. The following will match: **abxzy**, **abdcdccd**, **xzy**, **c**, and **cd**, but xzyc or cxzy will not.

Positionally, you do not have many options; you can specify whether the match should start at the beginning of the line (^), or it should match till the end of the line ($), or you do not care (no sign).

The `lookahead` and `lookbehind` options can be handy in certain situations too, but we will not cover them at this time.

> Beware. For certain patterns, the matching might take exponentially long; see `http://en.wikipedia.org/wiki/ReDoS` for examples. This might warn you to do not accept arbitrary regular expressions as a user input in your workflows.

Partial versus whole match

The pattern can be matched by two ways. You can test whether the whole text matches the pattern or just tries to find the matching parts within the text (probably multiple times). Usually, the partial match is used, but the whole match also has some use cases; for example, when you want to be sure that no remaining parts are present in the input.

Usage from Java

If you want to use regular expressions from Java, you have basically two options:

- Use `java.lang.String` methods
- Use `java.util.regex.Pattern` and related classes

In the first case, you have not much control about the details; for example, a `Pattern` object will be created for each call of the facade methods delegating to the `Pattern` class (methods such as `split`, `matches`, or `replaceAll`, `replaceFirst`). The usage of `Pattern` and `Matcher` allows you to write efficient (using `Pattern#compile`) and complex conditions and transformations. However, in both cases, you have to be careful, because the escaping rules of Java and the syntax of regular expressions do not make them an easy match. When you use \ in a regular expression within a string, you have to double them within the quotes, so you should write \\d instead of \d and \\\\ instead of \\ to match a single \.

> **Automate the escaping**
>
> The QuickREx tool (see *References, tools*) can do the escaping. You create the pattern, test it, navigate to **File | New... | Untitled Text File**, and select the **Copy RE to Java** action from the menu or the **QuickREx** toolbar. (Now you can copy the pattern to the clipboard and insert them anywhere you want and close the text editor.)

On the `Pattern` object, you can call the `matcher` method with the text as an argument and get a `Matcher` object. On the `Matcher` object, you can invoke either the `find` (for partial matches) or the `matches` (for whole matches) methods. As we described previously, you might have different results.

References and tools

- The Java tutorial about regular expressions might be a good starting point, and can be referred to at: `http://docs.oracle.com/javase/tutorial/essential/regex/index.html`

- The Javadoc of the `Pattern` class is a good summary and you can refer to it at: `http://docs.oracle.com/javase/7/docs/api/java/util/regex/Pattern.html`

- If you prefer testing the regular expressions, QuickREx is a good choice for eclipse (KNIME) and can be referred to at: `http://www.bastian-bergerhoff.com/eclipse/features/web/QuickREx/toc.html`

 There is a **Reg. Exp. Library** view that is also included in QuickREx.

Alternative pattern description

In KNIME, there is an alternative, simpler form of pattern description named **wildcard patterns**. These are similar to the DOS/Windows or UNIX shell script wildcard syntax. The * character matches zero or more characters (greedy match), but the ? character matches only a single character. The star and question mark characters cannot be used in patterns to match these characters.

Transforming the shape

There are multiple ways to change the shape of the data. Usually, it is just projection or filtering, but there are more complex options too.

Filtering rows

For row filters, the usual naming convention is used; that is, the node names ending with "Filter" give only a single table as a result, while the "Splitter" nodes generate two tables: one for the matches and one for the non-matching rows.

For single-column conditions, the **Row Filter** (and **Row Splitter**) node can be used to select rows based on a column value in a range, regular expression, or missing values. It is also possible to keep only these rows or filter these out. For row IDs, you can only use the regular expressions.

The rows can also be filtered by the (one-based) row index.

The **Nominal Value Row Filter** node gives a nice user interface when the possible values of textual columns are known at configuration time; so, you do not have to create complex regular expressions to match only those exact values.

There is a splitter, especially for numeric values, named **Numeric Row Splitter**. The configuration dialog allows you to specify the range's openness and gives better support for the variable handling than the **Row Splitter** node.

When you want to filter based on a date/time column, you should use the **Extract Time Window** node, which allows you to specify which time interval should be selected in the result table.

Imagine a situation where you already have a list of values that should be used as a filter for other tables; for example, you used HiLite to select certain values of a table. In this case, you can use one of this table's column to keep or remove the matching rows based on the other table's column. This can be performed by using the **Reference Row Filter** node. The **Set Operator** node is also an option to filter based on the reference table (Complement, Intersection, Exclusive-or), but in this case, you get only the selected columns and not the rest of the rows.

 Use the **Set Operator** node to create reference tables.

A very general option to filter rows is using either the **Java Snippet Row Filter** or the **Java Snippet Row Splitter** node. These are interpretations of Java (Boolean) expressions for each row, and based on these results the rows are included or excluded.

We have already introduced the **HiLite Filter** node in the previous chapter, which is also a row-filtering node.

Sampling

If you want to split the data for training, testing, or validation, you can use the **Partition** node that allows you to use the usual options for this purpose (such as stratified sampling). The filtering version is named **Row Sampling**. If you need sampling with replacement, you should use **Bootstrap Sampling**.

The **Equal Size Sampling** node tries to find a subset of rows that satisfies the condition of each value being represented (approximately or exactly) the same number of times as a given nominal column.

Appending tables

This node might not be so easy to find; it is named **Concatenate** or **Concatenate (Optional in)**. These nodes can be used to have two or more (up to four) tables' content in a new one. The handling of the row IDs and the different columns should be specified.

If the data you want to add is just the empty rows with the specified columns, **Add Empty Rows** will do that for you.

Less columns

Sometimes too much data can be distracting, or it might cause problems during modeling and transformation. For this reason, there are nodes to reduce the number of columns. In this section, we will introduce these nodes.

The **Column Filter** node is the most basic option to remove columns. You can specify which columns you want to keep or remove. A similar purpose node is the **Splitter** node. The only difference is that both parts will be available, but in different tables.

The **Reference Column Filter** node helps in creating similar tables, but you can also use this to remove common columns based on a reference table.

When you create a column to represent the reason for missing values, you might need to replace the original column's missing values with that reason. For this task, the **Column Merger** node can be used. It has the option to keep the original columns too.

When you want to have the values from different columns in a single collection column, you should use the **Create Collection Column** node. It can keep the original columns, but can also remove them. You can specify if you want to get the duplicate values removed, or if they should be kept in the selected columns.

Dimension reduction

Sometimes, you don't have a prior knowledge of which columns are useful and which are not. In these cases, the dimension reduction nodes are of great help.

The **Low Variance Filter** node keeps the original columns unless their variance is lower than a certain threshold (you can specify the variance threshold and the columns to check). Low variance might indicate that the column is not having an active role in identifying the samples.

When you want to select the columns based on the inter-column correlation, you should use the **Correlation Filter** node with the **Linear Correlation** node. The latter can compute the correlation between the selected columns, and the filter keeps only one of the highly correlated columns (for "high", you can specify a threshold).

The **Principal Component Analysis (PCA)** is a well-known dimension-reduction algorithm. KNIME's implementation allows you to invert the transformation (with errors if any information was omitted). The nodes are: **PCA** (computes and applies transformation based on threshold or number of dimensions), **PCA Compute** (computes the covariance matrix and the model), **PCA Apply** (applies the model with the settings), **PCA Inversion** (inverts the transformation).

The **multidimensional scaling (MDS)** operation is also a dimension-reduction algorithm. To use a fixed set of points/rows, you should use the **MDS Projection** node, but if you want to use data points automatically, the **MDS** node is your choice.

More columns

When you have columns that contain too much data in a structured form, you might want them being separated to new columns. You might also need to combine one data source with another; we will describe how to do this in this section.

The **Cell Splitter** node can create new columns from textual columns by splitting them using a delimiter text, while the **Cell Splitter By Position** node creates the new columns by the specified positions (and column names). The first node is useful when you have to do simple parsing, (for example, you read a table with tabs as separator characters, but the date field also uses a separator character, such as /, or -), but the second is better when you have a well-defined description with fixed length parts (like ISBN numbers or personal IDs).

With the **Regex Split** node, you can do more complex parsing of the data. Each capturing group can be extracted to a column. Keep in mind that for groups that have multiple matches, such as (...) +, only the last match will be returned, not all, or the first.

The **Column to Grid** node is used for moving data from rows to new columns in the order of the rows. It will remove the unselected columns, because those cannot be represented in this way, but the selected ones will contain the values from rows in the new columns.

A practical task is referring to previous rows. It is not impossible to achieve this with other nodes, but the **Lag Column** node makes this an easy task.

Finally, you can combine two tables using the **Joiner** node. It can perform inner, left, right, or outer joins, based on the row keys or columns. This way you can enrich your data from other data sources (or from the same data source if there are self-references). If you would like to join two tables based on the row indices (practically combine them in a new table horizontally), you should use the **Column Appender** node.

GroupBy

GroupBy is the most versatile data shaping node, even though it looks simple. You specify certain columns that should be used to group certain rows (when the values in the selected columns are the same in two rows, they will be in the same group) and compute aggregate values for the nongroup columns. These aggregation columns can be quite complex; for example, you might retain all the values if you create a list of them (almost works like pivoting). If you want to create a simple textual summary about the values, the **Unique concatenate with count** node might be a nice option for this purpose. If you want to filter out the infrequent or outlier rows/groups, you can compute the necessary statistics with this node. It is worth noting that there are special statistical nodes when you do not want to group certain rows. Check the **Statistics** category for details. However, you can also check the **Conditional Box Plot** node for robust estimates.

With the **Ungroup** node, you can reverse the effect of **GroupBy** transformations by creating collection columns; for example, if you generate the group count and the values in the first step, filtering out the infrequent rows will give you a table, which can be retransformed with the **Ungroup** node (assuming you need only a single column).

Simpler pivoting/unpivoting can be done this way.

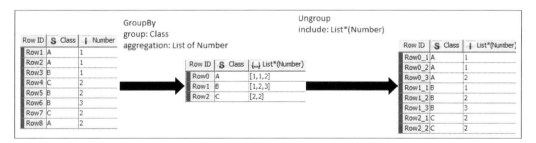

In the preceding screenshot, we start with a simple table, GroupBy using the Class column, and generate the list of values belonging to those classes, then we undo this transformation using the **Ungroup** node by specifying the collection column.

Pivoting and Unpivoting

The **Pivoting** node's basic option (when there is no actual pivoting) is the same as the **GroupBy** node. When you select the pivoting columns too, these columns will also act as grouping columns for their values; however, the values for group keys will not increase the number of rows, but multiply the number of columns for each aggregate option. The group totals and the whole table totals are also generated to separate the tables. The **Append overall totals** option has results in the Pivot totals table only.)

When you want to move the column headers to the rows and keep the values, **Unpivoting** will be your friend. With this node, the column names can be retrieved, and if you further process it using the **Regex Split** and **Split Collection Column** nodes, you can even reconstruct the original table to some extent.

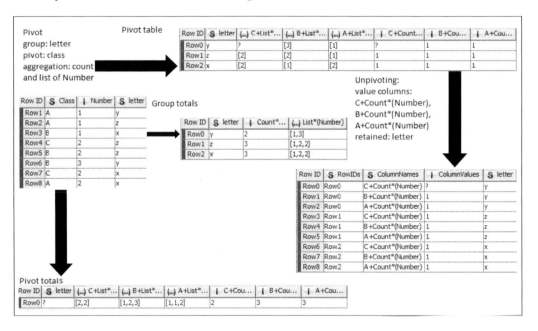

This time the initial table is a bit more complex, it has a new column, letter. The **Pivot** node used with the new column (letter) as grouping and the Class as pivot column. This time not just the list, but also the count of numbers are generated (the count is the most typical usage). The three output tables represent the results, while the table with the RowIDs column is the result when the **Unpivoting** node is used on the top result table with the count columns as values and the letter column retained.

One2Many and Many2One

Many modeling techniques cannot handle multinomial variables, but you can easily transform them to binomial variables for each possible value. To perform this task, you should use the **One2Many** node. Once you have created the model and applied it to your data, you might want to see the results according to their original values. With the **Many2One** node, this can be easily done if you have only one winner class label.

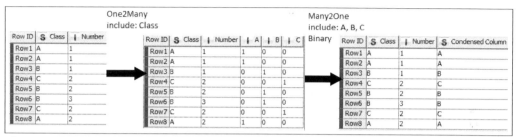

The **One2Many** node creates new columns with binary variables, while the **Many2One** can convert them back.

Cosmetic transformations

This section will summarize some of the options that are not so important for the data mining algorithms, but are important when you want to present the results to humans.

Renames

The **Extract Column Header** and **Insert Column Header** nodes can help you if you want to make multiple renames with a pattern in your mind. This way, you can extract the header, modify it as you want (for example, using another table's header as a reference), and insert the changed header to the result. For those places where a regular expression is suitable for automatic renames, the **Column Rename (Regex)** node can be used.

When a manual rename is easier, the **Column Rename** node is the best choice; it can even change the type of columns to more generic or compatible ones.

Changing the column order

The **Column Resorter** node can do what its name suggests. You can manually select the order you would prefer, but you can also specify the alphabetical order.

Reordering the rows

Using the **Sorter** node, you can order your data by the values of the selected column. Other columns can also be selected to handle ties.

When you want the opposite, for example, get a random order of rows, the **Shuffle** node will reorder them.

The row ID

The row ID, or row key, has an important role in the views, as in the tooltips, or as axis labels, where usually the row ID is used. With the **RowID** node, you can replace the current ID of rows based on column values, or create a column with the values of row ID. You can even test for duplication with this node by creating a row ID from that column. If there are duplicates, the node can fail or append a suffix to the generated ID depending on the settings.

When you use the row IDs to help HiLiting, the **Key-Collection HiLite Translator** node is useful if you have a column with a collection of strings, which are the row keys in the other table.

Transpose

The **Transpose** node simply switches the role of rows and columns and performs the mathematical transpose function on matrices. It is not a cosmetic transformation, although it can be seldom used to get better looking results. The type of the column is the most specific type available for the original row.

Transforming values

Sometimes the data that you have requires further processing; that is, not just moving around but also changing some values.

Generic transformations

A quite flexible node is the **Rule Engine** node that creates or replaces a column based on certain rules involving other columns. It might contain logical and relational operators for texts, and it can even check for inclusion (IN) for a certain set of values or limited pattern matching (LIKE as in SQL). The result can be either a constant, a column's value, or a flow variable. It can also handle the missing values.

When you want to fill the metadata, you should use the **Domain Calculator** node. With the help of this node, you can create nominal columns from textual (String) columns.

Java snippets

The most generic cell transformation nodes are the Java snippet nodes (**Java Snippet** and **Java Snippet (Simple)**). They allow you to use the third-party libraries, custom code to transform a row's values, or append new columns with those values. This is considered a last resort option though, because it makes it harder to get a visual overview of the workflow, when there are multiple snippet nodes used and requires Java knowledge of the user.

You have been warned, so now we can introduce how to use it when you need it.

Let us see what is in the configuration dialog:

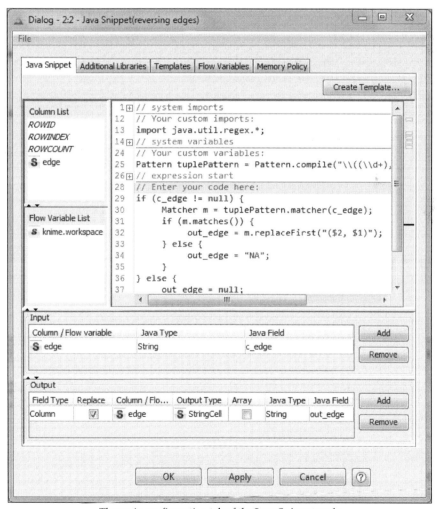

The main configuration tab of the **Java Snippet** node

As you can see, to the left of the window, there is a columns list and the flow variables list, while to the right you can see a coding area with the syntax highlighted (also code completion and error highlighting). Beneath them you can specify the values in the input and output columns. The output can be not only columns, but also the flow variables (With the simple version, you can only have a single column as the output). You can use the mouse to insert references to flow variables, columns, or row/table properties; just double-click them. The code completion can be activated using *Ctrl + spacebar* or just waiting after writing a method/field selector (.) for an object.

In the coding area, the menu which appears on right-clicking also works, just like the undo (*Ctrl+Z*)/redo (*Ctrl+Y*) commands. Some of the parts of the surrounding code are hidden (folded) initially, but if you are curious, you can see them.

The regular exceptions are swallowed, so it will not stop the execution; however, missing cells and null flow variables will be created for that row. If you want to stop the execution, you should throw an Abort exception.

When you do not want to import a reference to a certain column or flow variable, you use the snippets methods, which are described in the node description at: http://www.knime.org/files/nodedetails/_misc_java_snippet_Java_ Snippet.html.

 You can declare custom variables as static fields, but those will not retain their values after a reset, so you will not gain too much (and static fields can be seen as a bad practice).

In the **Additional Libraries** tab, you can specify which jars should also be loaded for this snippet. This way, you can use quite complex libraries besides the standard Java Runtime Environment.

The **Templates** tab allows you to load a template from the available repositories. You can create your own using the **Create Template...** button on the main tab of the **Java Snippet** configuration.

The flow control category contains similar, yet specialized, nodes to change flow variables named **Java Edit Variables** and **Java Edit Variables (simple)**, but as a row filter, you can either use **Java Snippet Row Filter** or **Java Snippet Row Splitter**.

The Math Formula node

The **KNIME Math Expression (JEP)** extension is available from the standard KNIME update site and adds the **Math Formula** node to the repository.

The **Math Formula** node is similar to the **String Manipulation** node, but it works with numbers and not with texts. Here you also have different kinds of composable functions and a few helper variables and constants. The following are the main categories of functions:

- Trigonometric
- Logarithmic/exponential
- Rounding
- Statistical
- Other (rand, abs, sqrt, if, and binom)

Using these functions, you can transform the values from a row without knowing the Java syntax.

Conversion between types

We previously mentioned that "upcasting" can be performed using the **Column Rename** node, although usually we are not that lucky to have only that kind of transformation. If you want to sort the numeric data by their textual representation (for example, "1"<"10"<"2"), the **Number To String** node will help to do that. (Unfortunately, you cannot specify precision or number format this way. The format uses scientific notation (no thousands separators) and use point (.) as a decimal delimiter.) Another use case might be needed to append the units to the number.

> **Round before converting to text**
> Using the **Round Double** node, you can remove the noise of too precise values if you want to show the converted values in a better way.

The **Round Double** node allows you to select the precision and the rounding mode, and can convert to the data to textual format, but can keep the floating point representation too. When you convert to text, it might not use the scientific notation; so, it might suit your needs better in certain cases.

The other way, using the **String To Number** node, you can specify whether you want to parse the values as floating point numbers or integers. You can also set what should be the decimal and the thousands separator.

Another option to convert the textual column values to numbers is using the **Category To Number** and apply helper nodes, **Category To Number (Apply)**, if you want to use the same transformation on a different table. These are creating a transformation (PMML) model, which specifies which numbers should be assigned to certain values of the selected textual columns.

The **Double To Int** node can be used to convert the floating point numbers to integers. You can select the columns and the rounding mode.

When you have (hexadecimal or binary) numbers represented as a text, or the bit positions separated by spaces, you can create a bitvector from them using the **Bitvector Generator** node. You can also use this node to assign 0 or 1 to each selected numeric columns based on a fix separator value or relative to the mean of the individual columns. These values are then combined to bitvectors.

The **String to Date/Time** and the **Time to String** nodes allow you to convert between dates and texts. You can specify the date format in both cases, but you cannot set the locale.

With the **Column To XML** node, you can convert multiple columns (row-wise) to a single XML column, and the **XPath** node can extract information from XML cells as texts. If you want to parse an XML document from a text column to the KNIME XML data type, you should use the **String To XML** node.

Binning

When your preferred modeling algorithm cannot handle the numeric classes, but there are too many values to use them for classification without overfitting, a good option is creating intervals (bins) based on the values, and using those interval labels (or their **One2Many** variables) for learning. Fortunately, KNIME has good tools to solve this problem too.

First of all, you should decide whether you want to specify the boundaries manually, or an automatic way is preferred. If you want manual bins, the **Numeric Binner** node should be used. This node allows you to set the different ranges for selected numeric columns in the configuration dialog. If you have a mapping already available as a table, you should use the **Binner (Dictionary)** node. The rule table should contain the label and the lower and the upper bounds (you cannot specify for each rule how the end points of the interval should be included for the rule set).

The automatic binning construction can be done using the **Auto-Binner** node. You can specify how many bins you want or just select the percentiles for the bin boundaries. With the **Auto-Binner (Apply)** node, you can use the result of that binning in other tables or columns, but in this case the boundary labels could be misleading if there are values outside the original interval.

The other options for automatic binning are the **CAIM Binner** and **CAIM Applier** nodes. These nodes learn binning based on a class label column that tries to minimize the class interdependency measure.

Normalization

Several algorithms do not work well when the range of the numeric values are on a different scale. Think of those that use a difference metric. In such cases, a relatively large change in a variable with small range is not recognizable. For this reason, KNIME supports normalization of values using the **Normalizer** node, which also creates a transformation model that can be applied to other tables using the **Normalizer (Apply)** node. You can select from three different normalization methods as follows:

- Min-max
- Z-score
- Decimal scaling

The min-max normalization scales the values to a user-defined range, while Z-score will transform the values such that the mean will be zero and the standard deviation will be one. Decimal scaling converts the values such that they are not larger than one in their absolute values. This is achieved by finding the smallest power of 10 that satisfies this condition.

The **Denormalizer** node inputs a model from **Normalizer** and applies its inverse version on the data. This way, you can show the data in the original range.

Text normalization

Not only the numeric values should be normalized, but also the text in columns might need some further processing. For this purpose, you can use the **Cell Replacer**, **String Replacer**, **String Replace (Dictionary)**, **Case Converter**, and **String Manipulation** nodes. The **Rule Engine** node can also be used for related tasks, while the **Missing Value** node can be used to specify alternative values for the missing values.

The **Cell Replacer** node is a general whole-content replacer node (or appends for certain preferences). You have to specify a dictionary table and the column to change. In the dictionary table, you also have to select the two columns (from and to).

This functionality is a little bit similar to the **String Replace (Dictionary)** node; however, in the **String Replace (Dictionary)** node, the input is not another table, but a file similar to prolog rules, where the term to generate is the first, whereas the conditions are the rest. Although, unlike prolog, the conditions are "or"-ed, not "and"-ed in the same rows; so, if any of the keys match, the head will be used as a replacement. You can think of this as an ordinary dictionary table that was grouped by the replacement values. This can be a compact form of the rules, although you still can have multiple rows with the same replacement (first column) values.

The **String Replacer** node can be handy when you want to replace only certain parts of the input text. It uses the wildcard pattern or regular expressions. You can replace the whole string or just the parts that match.

The **Case Converter** node can do a simple task; that is, normalize the texts to all uppercase or to all lowercase.

The **String Manipulation** node, on the other hand, can do that and much more with texts. You can use multiple (even non-textual) columns in the expression that generate a result (which can also be not just text but logical or numeric values too). The functions which you can use fall into the following categories:

- Change case
- Comparison
- Concatenate
- Convert type
- Count
- Extract
- Miscellaneous (only reverse yet)
- Remove
- Replace
- Search

These functions cannot handle date and time or collection values; however, for positional or exact matches, these are great tools as they allow you to compose the provided functions.

Regular expressions

With the **Java Snippet** node, you can perform the changes using regular expressions too. Here is an example of the code snippet:

```java
// system imports
// Your custom imports:
import java.util.regex.*;
// system variables
// Your custom variables:
Pattern tuplePattern = Pattern.compile("\\((\\d+),\\s*(\\d+)\\)");
// expression start
// Enter your code here:
if (c_edge != null) {
  Matcher m = tuplePattern.matcher(c_edge);
```

```
  if (m.matches()) {
    out_edge = m.replaceFirst("($2, $1)");
  } else {
    out_edge = "NA";
  }
} else {
  out_edge = null;
}
// expression end
```

The automatically generated parts are hidden in this code. We have the c_edge field as an input and out_edge as an output. First, we import the Pattern and Matcher classes using the import statement. The pattern we used translates to the following: find an opening parenthesis, then a nonnegative integer number (within a group, so it is interesting for us, which is group number 1), a comma, possibly a few white spaces, another nonnegative number (also interesting, group number 2), and closing parenthesis. You might notice that to escape the \ character, we had to double them between the quotes.

For each row's edge text, we test whether the edge is missing or not. After that, we check (when not missing) whether it fully matches our pattern; if yes, we replace the whole matching pattern with the opening parenthesis, the second number ($2), a comma, a space, and the first number ($1) followed by a closing parenthesis. If there is no proper match, we return NA, but if it is missing, we return the missing value (null).

You can see this code in action if you import the project from ReverseEdges.zip.

It is worth noting that such a similar task can be more easily done with the **String Replacer** node, but this technique can be used in more complex cases too, and can be a template for extension.

Multiple columns

When you want to create a single value from multiple columns, you have several options: **Column Aggregator**, **Column Combiner**, **Column Merger**, and **Create Collection Column**.

The **Create Collection Column** option is quite specific and does what its name suggests. The **Column Aggregator** option can do the same function as The **Create Collection Column** option and also various other aggregation methods, such as computing statistics, summarizing the selected columns, or performing set operations among collections. For details about the available functions, check its **Description** tab.

When you just want a single string from multiple columns, you should use the **Column Combiner** option. You can set the parameters to make it reversible for text values.

The **Column Merger** node is useful when you want to merge two columns, based on the presence of values; for example, imagine the state and country columns for persons. When a country has no states, you might want the country name present in the state column too (or you might want to keep only the state column with the country value if it was missing previously). It is easy to solve using this node.

We already mentioned the **Many2One** node during structural transformations, but it is worth referring to that here too. You can create a single column from the binary columns with at most one inclusion value.

XML transformation

The XML transformation nodes are a part of the **KNIME XML-Processing** extension, available from the standard KNIME update site.

With the **XML Column Combine** node, you can create new XML values row-wise from the existing XML columns. In case you do not have XML values yet, you can still create a new value with custom or data bound attributes for each row.

To create a single XML from a column's values, you should use the **XML Row Combine** node. This can be useful when you want to generate parts for the XLSX or ODS files. With the file handling nodes, you can replace data within templates.

There are Java libraries that can be used to transform XML content or even HTML; for example, Web-Harvest (http://web-harvest.sourceforge.net/index.php). These libraries are useful when something complex should be performed, but for standard transformation tasks, the **XSLT** node is sufficient. It can collect values/ parts from the XML values; so, it is a form of extraction and search too, just like the **XPath** node.

Time transformation

When you have too many details available, it might be hard to focus on the important parts. In case of dates, you might be not interested in the actual time of day, the actual day, month, or year, or the date is not important, because all of your data points are within a day. We can split the date column to have this information in separate (numeric valued) columns using the **Date Field Extractor** and the **Time Field Extractor** nodes.

The **Mask Date/Time** node does a similar thing, but it works on the time column and keeps/removes the time of day, the date, or the milliseconds information (but only one at a time).

With **Preset Date/Time**, you can specify the removed/missing parts of the date or time to a preset value, but you can also use this node to set the date/time values for missing values.

Computing the difference between the dates and time is a common task. With the **Time Difference** node, you can not only find out the difference in various units between two columns, but also a fixed date (and time), or the current time, or the previous row.

Smoothing

Using the **Moving Average** node, we can smooth the numeric values using a date/time column. It can use various methods to compute the moving average; the node description introduces them with the formulae.

Data generation

There is a KNIME Labs plug-in named **KNIME Datageneration** (`http://tech.knime.org/datageneration`). It gives support to generate values from different distributions for existing rows to new columns:

- **Random Number Assigner**: It supports uniform distribution
- **Gaussian Distributed Assigner**: It supports Gaussian distribution
- **Beta Distributed Assigner**: It supports beta distribution
- **Gamma Distributed Assigner**: It supports gamma distribution

To generate rows with numeric content, the most obvious node is **Data Generator**. It generates data for clusters of normally distributed data for various dimensions with different cluster centers on the `[0,1]` interval. It also generates the cluster labels.

To generate empty rows for existing tables, the **Add Empty Rows** node gives options. You might also want to create a table specification before you add (new or additional) empty rows. This can be done using the **Create Table Structure** or the **Table Creator** nodes. Both are manual, but if you have a tab/comma-separated file with the header, it might be easier to read that file using the **File Reader** node.

If you have a table with empty rows, you can use the **Java Snippet** node to generate sequences or grids to that table. You can see the idea in action in the workflow from the `GenerateGrid.zip` file.

The **Time Generator** node allows you to generate rows with equidistant values with a single date column between two dates.

You can also use the **Empty Table Creator** node from the data generation plug-in to generate empty rows without columns

The **SMOTE** node fills the spare parts of a class of rows with new rows. It uses an algorithm to generate similar rows to previously existing ones in a class based on their numeric attributes.

Generating the grid

We created a workflow which demonstrates how we can generate a grid with equidistant points in each dimension. In this section, we will introduce some of the details of this workflow. You can import the workflow from the GenerateGrid. zip file.

First of all, you have to set the column structure and the parameters of the grid. The column names should match in the **Parameters** node's colName column and the **Empty structure** node columns.

Description of the **Parameters** node columns are as follows:

- colName: The name of the column to be generated
- numberOfPoints: Specifies the number of points that will be generated for that dimension (including end points)
- minValue, maxValue: Specifies the two end points of the closed intervals

In the **Generate Grid** meta node, first (**Java Snippet** and **helper columns**), we generate a few auxiliary values. The product of the number of points will be used to find out how many rows should be generated, while the modulo will be used to compute the row index's range for the column.

Next, we find out how many rows should be generated, by sorting in descending order, based on the cumulativeProduct column and then converting the first row to a workflow variable.

Using this variable, we add new empty rows to the table (**Add Empty Rows**).

Now, we have to create an expression using the **String Manipulator** node, for each parameter row, to generate the Java snippet formula. Fortunately, we have the ROWINDEX information available when we use the $$ROWINDEX$$ expression. Here is the whole expression of the node:

```
join("return ($$ROWINDEX$$ / ", string($modulo$), " % ",
    string($numberOfPoints$), " / (", string($numberOfPoints$), " -
    1.0)) * (", string($maxValue$), " - ", string($minValue$), ") +
    ", string($minValue$), ";")
```

It could have been easier if we used the **Java Snippet** node, but because this is just concatenating few values, it was a more consistent option, and we can use this opportunity to introduce a few **String Manipulator** functions. The join function just concatenates its arguments, but it assumes all of them are textual. For this reason, our numeric values are converted to text using the string function.

An example expression might look like the following after the execution of the function:

```
return ($$ROWINDEX$$ / 7 % 11 / (11 - 1.0)) * (30.0 - 10.0) +
    10.0;
```

The number 7 is the modulo value, 11 is the number of points (*n*), and 1.0 is an adjustment constant (the length of the [0, n-1] interval is n-1, which is the reason for this constant), which also converts the expression to double, but 30.0 and 10.0 are the maximum and minimum end points of the interval of the current column.

 Please note these expressions are for Java snippets (simple version), although, you could also use the **Math Formula** node later with little modifications.

The remaining part of the meta node is a loop over the extended parameters data table (**TableRow To Variable Loop Start**); however, the content is not collected in new rows for the consecutive runs, but in the columns (because we used the **Loop End (Column Append)** looping node). We have to keep only the target column from the original table, else the column names would generate conflict during the loop end node's column append step, and these would be renamed. For this reason, we used the **Column Filter** node. The final step within the loop is generating the value we want in the target column for the specified rows using the **Java Snippet (Simple)** node.

In the end, you get a grid which looks like the following screenshot (the y-z projection of it):

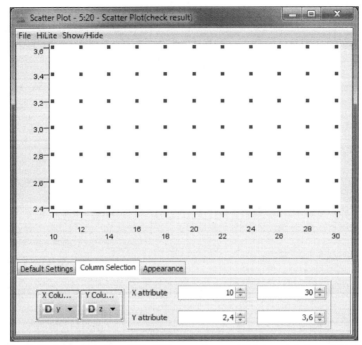

A generated grid with 11 data points from 10 to 30 for y values and 7 data points from 2.4 to 3.6 on the z axis.

Exercise
Modify the workflow to use not the number of points for each dimension but the distance of the adjacent points! The bounds are still required.

The final node of the workflow is the **Scatter Plot** node to visualize (and check) the results.

Constraints

You can seldom trust the data you have because there can be network problems during import, or the program that was generated was wrongly parameterized, the program got invalid input, or the device you used to collect the data was used out of its operating conditions. For these reasons, it is a good practice to find constraints and check them after import or more complex transformations. You should also check the user input, and if it might cause hard-to-discover problems in later phases, report them as soon as you can.

The **Flow Control/Switches** nodes can be used to enable the workflow parts selectively (this is useful if the check of constraints is not always required, or it is too time consuming to be on by default or to try correcting the wrong data), but the loop-related nodes (**Flow Control/Loop Support**) are also useful when multiple columns should be tested and can handle complex conditions.

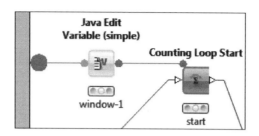

In the preceding screenshot, a flow variable comes from outside of the meta node, the **Java Edit Variable (simple)** node transforms it, and the result goes to the **Counting Loop Start** node, where it can be used to set the parameters.

The **IF Switch** node is not really helpful in this regard, but when you create mock/ artificial test data you can specify whether that should be merged to the normal data or not. The actual merge can be done by either the **End IF** node or one of the **Concatenate** nodes.

The **CASE Switch** node works similarly with just three possible states (outputs) and better support for workflow variables in the switch condition. The join operation of the case switch can be performed to signal possible errors (**End (Model) CASE**) when there are more than one active branches, or just concatenate them (**End CASE**).

The **Java IF** node and the **Empty Table Switch** node are more automated. They depend on the state of the input on the branching node too, not just during the join. The latter simply forwards the data to the first output port if the input is not empty (has rows), else it forwards the data to the second output port. On the other hand, the **Java IF** node can use flow variables and other states (such as the current date and the random number generators) to select the first or second port as the destination for the input.

For example, when you remove the rows that contain missing values and no rows remain, the **Empty Table Switch** node might give you an alternative path to handle that situation, and yet finish the execution of the workflow. The **Row Filter** node can also be used in combination with it to check whether a certain number of rows are available or not.

When you want to signal an error, the best option is the **Breakpoint** node because it was designed for this purpose. You specify whether an empty table, an active or inactive branch, or a certain flow variable value is the erroneous condition, and if it is satisfied, the execution of the node will fail.

The **Try** and **Catch Errors** family of nodes in the **Error Handling** category is useful when you want to handle the failures of the nodes in an alternative way.

Obviously, a **Java Snippet** node can be used to signal an error if the condition does not require more context than a row, but it is not ideal to collect the "bad" rows. For this purpose, the **Java Snippet Row Filter** node is a better choice. When it is combined with the previous constructs, you can create complex error-handling scenarios.

Some of the metadata of a table can be converted to another table using the **Extract Table Dimension** and the **Extract Table Spec** nodes. The former just computes how many rows and columns are there, but the latter extracts the min-max values, types, and column names for the input table.

The **Set Operator** node can be used to compare different tables; for example, if you have possibly removed the rows (with the **Missing Values** node), you can check whether the difference to the original table is an empty table or not with the **Breakpoint** node.

Loops

Doing the same thing multiple times might look like a bad idea, but we usually are doing slightly different things in each iteration, and with loops, we can factor out the repetition, and our workflows are easily reused.

A few notes about the loops:

- The flow variables that they generate are read-only; when you replace them, you do not modify them (as those are handled internally), just hide them from further processing
- The loops can be nested, so it is possible to have things done quite a lot of times

The simple **Counting Loop Start** node just feeds the same input table (as many times as specified) to the loop, each time increasing the `currentIteration` flow variable.

When you would like to iterate without the `[0, maxIteration-1]` interval or the preferred increment is not one, you should consider using the **Interval Loop Start** node instead of the counting.

Iterating through a table and splitting the input table to smaller chunks can be useful when it is too large to handle it with the workflow; however, it can also be used to make sure that certain parts are analyzed independently. With the **Chunk Loop Start** node, the data will be split to parts with *n* rows, or they will be split to *n* parts depending on the configuration. When you want to group the rows, not by their order, but by their values in certain columns and use those chunks for processing, you should use the **Group Loop Start** node.

With the **Column List Loop Start** node, you can go through the selected columns of the input table without extracting them in the table. An alternative is using the **TableRow To Variable Loop Start** node and the **Extract Table Spec** node. Both looping nodes keep not just the current iteration number in a workflow variable, but other information too (the column name in the former case or the row's actual values in the latter).

The **Generic Loop Start** node can be thought of as a `do ... while` loop's `do` part. It is just a delimiter of the loop. The `while` part is the **Variable Condition Loop End** node.

When you use the **Loop End** node to signal the end of a loop, the generated tables (the input of this node) will be concatenated, and if that is not possible (for example, incompatible columns are generated), it will fail. When you want to have your generated columns available, you should end the loop with the **Loop End (Column Append)** node (the tables are joined by their row IDs, so be sure they are compatible in this case).

In cases where you need to return multiple tables from the loop, the previous loop end options are not satisfactory; however; the **Loop End (2 Ports)** node enables you to collect the tables from two sources and return them separately.

The **Variable Loop End** is useful when you do not have any tables to collect, because it does not accept tables as input. It returns the variables for each iteration, so it can be useful when you are debugging a looping flow.

Workflow customization

It is highly recommended to install the **KNIME Nodes to create KNIME Quick Forms** extension from the standard KNIME update site, because its nodes allow you to create configuration points for a whole part of your workflow. This way, your users can customize their needs more easily or just experiment with different parameters.

Here comes a short introduction to the **Quick Form** nodes. First, we will group these by what kind of information is generated:

- **Boolean Input**: It generates logical information
- **Integer Input**: It generates integer number
- **Double Input**: It generates double number
- **Date (String) Input**: It generates date (as text)
- **Column Filter QuickForm** (multiple column names; results in an empty table) **Column Selection QuickForm** (single column name): These generate date (as text)
- **String Input** (single line), **String Radio Buttons**, **Single Selection Input QuickForm** (single choice from enumerated possible values), **Multiple Selection Input QuickForm** (multiple choice from enumerated possible values, returns a table), **Variable Selection QuickForm** (single selection from the values of a nominal column), **Variable Filter QuickForm** (multiple selection from the values of a nominal column), **and Molecule String Input** (designed for molecules, although it does not check correctness in the KNIME Desktop): These generate text

On the KNIME web portal, these can be represented as different controls. For this reason, you can specify the label to show their description and the flow variable name in each of the previously introduced nodes.

You can configure the actual values of the QuickForms nodes by configuring the workflow or even the meta node. You can also use the **QuickForm Execution...** option to specify their values before executing the workflow.

Case study – finding min-max in the next n rows

In the next few sections, we will introduce some problems and our solution to them using KNIME.

Sometimes you are fine with the moving average for date type values, but in certain situations, you need the range of values for a window. In the workflow available in the `sliding_minmax.zip` file, we will do exactly this. We are assuming an equidistant distribution of date values in the rows; you can try to generalize to remove this restriction.

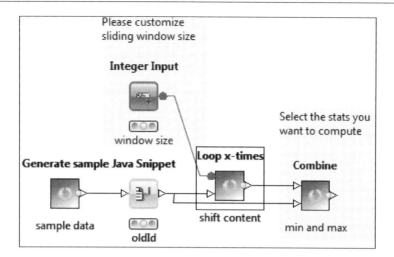

In the preceding screenshot, first (after generating some sample data) we add an ID based on the row index, then shift the content by the specified value in the **Integer Input** node, and finally combine the tables to find min and max values.

The main idea we use is described in the following steps: create a new table for each position in the sliding window (each shifted according to the position), and combine these tables using an identifier. Finally, we use the **GroupBy** node to select the values. Alternatively, we could also use the **Group Loop Start** node, but that would be quite slow and harder to understand. However, if you have to calculate the unsupported aggregation option(s), you should use the looping construct.

Let's see the details. The sample data was generated using the **Data Generator** node and the **Java Snippet** node. The latter was adding a column with daily time information to the generated table. If those were not equidistant consecutive dates, you should sort the table and fill the holes with, for example, the **SMOTE** node.

The **Integer Input** quick form node allows you to specify the window size easily, because we are using flow variables for this purpose. You might also create a meta node from the part that computes the statistics and wrap it around with a (counting) loop to try multiple options for the parameter.

We generate an integer ID to make it easy to combine the shifted tables later; this is quite simple. We could also use the **Math Formula** node, but to reduce the dependencies, we used the **Java Snippet** node with the row index as the values.

You should compute a different ID for non-equidistant values, but that would also require collecting certain statistics. In that case, finding the ID for the shifted values would also be harder.

In the loop meta node (**shift content**), we first decrease the window size variable, because the first shift is the no shift (that is, the original table), but the **Row Filter** node does not support filtering by position, so we will have to generate the shifted values and concatenate it to the result of the loop. In the loop, we delete the first *n* (currentIteration) row and assign it a new ID. The **Loop End** node will take care of the concatenation of the tables.

Simplify

Simplify the workflow with the **Lag Column** node. It was designed to perform a task similar to the meta node named shift content.

We add the original table to the shifted ones as the last step in the **Shift and combine** custom meta node.

To summarize the values in the sliding window, we use the **GroupBy** node. You might think it would be very laborious to set all of these columns for the minimum and the maximum too, but the KNIME configuration dialog is user-friendly and makes this easy.

- In the **Groups** tab, select only the ID column (old_id in this case) for inclusion
- In the **Options** tab, select **add all >>**, right-click on them, and select **Minimum** from the context menu
- Now, select **add all >>** again, select the new aggregation columns, and from the context menu, select **Maximum**.

Now everything is configured and ready to start.

Exercise

Would you prefer other ways of sliding windows? I do. We implemented the analogous version of the Forward simple method of the **Moving Average** node. Can you construct a Backward simple method? What about a Center simple method? It would be nice if the user could select between these methods using a **String Radio Buttons** node.

We hope you will find the trick useful to shift the rows. It can be useful in other situations too.

Case study – ranks within groups

In this case, we will compute ranks (based on a certain order) within groups. This is a much easier task, but can be very useful if you want to select the outliers without prior knowledge to define cut-off points. However, it can also be useful for summarizing historical data (find the three/five top hits leading the sales list the longest in different genres, for example). There is also a simplification when we do not need the rank, but just the extreme values. But, certain algorithms can use the rank values for better predictions, because we humans are biased to the best options. For example, in a 100-minute race, the difference between the first and the fifth drivers, is one minute hypothetically; that is it amounts to one percent. It's a quite small difference, although the difference in the prizes and fame are much larger.

The example workflow is in the `GroupRanks.zip` file.

First, we generate some sample data with the **Data Generator** node, just like before. Then we loop through the groups defined by the `Cluster Membership` column in the **Rank** custom meta node using the **Group Loop Start** looping node.

In the group, we sort the data by the `Universe_0_0` column in the ascending order (and the other numeric columns to break ties) with the **Sorter** node.

The **Java Snippet** node just uses the `ROWINDEX` method to calculate the result (the index + 1 to start ranking from one).

In the **Loop End** node, we disabled the generation of the iteration column, because it is not interesting for us, and the `Cluster Membership` column identifies the groups with a nice label.

That's it. This is really easy.

Exercise

Modify the example to give ranks from the opposite direction too. How would you do that without resorting to the subtable? Could you do it in a way that the small absolute ranks would be extreme values, while the larger ones are the usual? For example, 1, 2, 3, 4, -4, -3, -2, -1

Sometimes the rows that are outliers in multiple dimensions can be explained with a covariance between the columns. However, when you have other outliers, which are outliers only in a few dimensions, those might be a measure error in that column.

Exercise

Compute the ranks for a user-defined list of numeric columns in both directions to find outliers with this method.

With the ranks in the columns, you can now perform the checks you find worth executing.

Summary

In this chapter, we have constructed KNIME workflows to work with various data sources (generated, Internet, file, and database). We introduced the most important nodes to transform and preprocess the data we have. We have also combined this knowledge to implement solutions to different problems. By now, you would have an idea of how to construct KNIME workflows and how to use the flow variables and the loops.

3
Data Exploration

In this chapter, we will go through the main functions of KNIME visualization (except reporting) and other techniques to explore the data you have. This can be helpful when you want to do the preprocessing too, but you can also check the result of visualization or see how well they fit the computed models and the test/validation data. The topics covered in this chapter are as follows:

- Statistics
- Distance matrix
- Visual properties
- KNIME views and HiLiting
- JFreeChart nodes
- Some third party visualization options
- Tips with HiLiting
- Visualizing models

Computing statistics

When you want to explore your data, it usually is a good idea to compute some statistics about them so that you can spot the obviously wrong data (for example, when some data should be positive and it appears as a negative minimal value, it is suspicious).

Most of the nodes require you to not have NaN values within the data to be analyzed. You can remove them with the value modification techniques presented in the previous chapter, or by filtering the rows, also discussed in the previous chapter.

The minimal and maximal values can be checked in the port view's **Spec Columns** tab. This can already be used to spot certain kinds of problems.

For statistics within groups, we have the good old **GroupBy** node. That allows you to aggregate using the functions described on the **Description** tab of the configuration dialog.

When you do not need the grouping, you can use the **Statistics** node with easier configuration. Just select the columns, the number of values that should be present in the view, and the number of common/rare values that should be enumerated. You might find that the median is not computed in the results. In this case, you should check the **Calculate median values (computationally expensive)** checkbox. The following is the statistics you get in the view (for the numeric columns):

- **Minimum**
- **Maximum**
- **Mean**
- **Std deviation**
- **Variance**
- **Overall sum**
- **No. missings**
- **Median**
- **Row count**

You also get the number of missing values and the most common and rarest values for the selected nominal (and also numeric) columns, with their number of occurrences.

The statistics table, which is the first output port, contains the same content as the view for the numeric columns. The second output port (occurrences table) gives a table with the number of occurrences for each numeric and nominal values in a decreasing order of frequencies (including the missing values).

Using the output tables, you can create conditions or further aggregate operations. For example, creating the flow variables from the certain mean and standard deviation and creating conditions using the **Java Edit Variable** node allows you to filter the rows with certain ranges related to the mean and standard deviation with the row filtering/splitting nodes. (Or use the **Java Snippet Row Filter** node directly with the flow variables.)

The **Value Counter** node acts in a manner similar to the **Statistics** node's second output, but in this case, only a single column is used. So, no missing values will appear in the count column (which is not sorted) and the values from the original column will appear as row IDs. In this form, they are better suited for visualization. Also, because this node is able to support HiLite, you can select the original rows based on the frequency values.

When you want a similar (frequency) report with two columns and a possible weight column to create crosstabs, you should use the **Crosstab** node. In the view of the node, you get the crosstab values in the usual form. You can specify which parts (**Frequency, Expected, Deviation, Percent, Row Percent, Column Percent**, or **Cell Chi-Square**) should be visible. (The row and column totals are always visible, and if there are too many rows or columns, you can keep only the first few.)

There is another table in the view, beneath the frequency. It is the summary of the Chi-Square statistics (degree of freedom (DF), the χ^2 Value, and the probability (Prob) of no association between the values (a p-value)), and also the Fischer test's probability, when both columns contain exactly two values.

The **Crosstab** node's first output port contains the values similar to the view's main table, but in this case, it is in a different form: the column values are in columns, while the statistics (Frequency, Expected, Deviation, Percent, Row Percent, Column Percent, Total Row Count, Total Column Count, Total Count, and Cell Chi-Square) are in other columns. You can transform it to the usual crosstab form (keeping a single statistics) using the **Pivoting** node (select one of the columns as the group column, the other as pivot, and the statistics should be used as an aggregation option). You can check the workflow from the `crosstab.zip` file available on this book's website.

The second output table of the **Crosstab** node contains the statistics just like the second part of the view, but in this case it is in a single row even if both the columns contain two values (the Fischer test's p-value is in the last column).

When you want to create a correlation matrix, you should use the **Linear Correlation** node. It will compute the correlation between the numeric-numeric and nominal-nominal pairs. Also, a model will be created for further processing. You can use this information to reduce the number of columns with the help of the **Correlation Filter** node.

The view of the **Linear Correlation** node gives an overview about the correlation values with the color codes.

There are three t-test computing nodes: **Single sample t-test, Independent groups t-test**, and **Paired t-test**. The **Single sample t-test** can be used to test whether the average of the selected columns is a specified value or not. The **t-value (t)**, **degree of freedom (df)**, **p-value (2-tailed)**, **Mean Difference**, and **confidence interval differences** are computed relative to the specified mean value (the **Test value**). The other output table contains some statistics about the columns, such as the computed mean, standard deviation, standard error mean, and the number of missing values in that column.

The view of **Single sample t-test** contains the same information as the two output tables.

When you want to compare the means of two measurements of the same population (or at least not independent), you can use the **Paired t-test** node. The view and the resulting tables contain the same statistics as the **Single sample t-test** node, but in this case the mean difference is replaced with the standard deviation and the standard error mean values, both in the view and the first output table. The configuration options allow you to select multiple pairs of numeric columns.

For two sample t-tests, you should use the **Independent groups t-test** node. It expects the two groups to be defined by a column; the values are grouped by that column's values. You can select the column that contains the class for grouping and the values/labels for the two groups within that column. The average of the columns will be compared, and the t-tests will be computed both for the equal variance assumption and without that assumption (first output table). The Levene test is also computed to help decide whether the equal variance can be assumed (second output table).

The descriptive statistics is augmented with the number of rows that are not in either group (`Ignored Count (Group Column)`).

The last test for hypothesis testing is the **One-way ANOVA**. It allows you to compare the means within groups defined by the values of a single column, just like the **Independent groups t-test** node does; however, it supports multiple groups.

Finally, when you need robust statistics, you can use the **Conditional Box Plot** node. It gives you the minimum and maximum values, the median, Q1, Q3, and the whisker values (can be the same as min/max, else the 1.5 times interquartile range (Q3 – Q1) below or above Q1 and Q3).

Overview of visualizations

The various options to visualize data in KNIME allow you to get an overview or even publication-quality figures from the data you have preprocessed and analyzed.

The interactive versions of a node allow you to change the column selections and probably the other extra options.

The **JFreeChart** nodes generate images from the input data, which is also available as a view with further customization options. These nodes usually do not support the HiLite feature and the different visual properties (color, size, and shape).

First, to help decide what you use to open the data, we will compare the capabilities of the different visualization nodes:

Node	Supported data types	Remarks
Box Plot	Numeric (multiple)	Provides robust stats
Conditional Box Plot	Nominal and numeric (multiple)	Also gives robust stats
Histogram	Nominal or numeric and numeric	
Histogram (interactive)	Nominal or numeric and numeric	
Interactive Table	Any	Similar to port view
Lift Chart	Nominal and probability	
Line Plot	Numeric (multiple)	
Parallel Coordinates	Nominal or numeric	
Pie chart	Nominal and numeric	
Pie chart (interactive)	Nominal and numeric	
Scatter Matrix	Nominal or numeric	Multiple scatter plots
Scatter Plot	Nominal or numeric (two)	
Bar Chart (JFreeChart)	Nominal	
Bubble Chart (JFreeChart)	Numeric (three)	
Group By Bar Chart (JFreeChart)	Nominal (unique) and numeric	Color properties supported
HeatMap (JFreeChart)	Distance or numeric	Distance between rows
Interval Chart (JFreeChart)	Date and nominal	
Line Chart (JFreeChart)	Numeric (multiple) or date	Color properties supported
Pie Chart (JFreeChart)	Nominal	Color properties supported
Scatter Plot (JFreeChart)	Numeric (two)	Color, shape used
Linear Regression (Learner)	Numeric (multiple)	Scatter + line of model
Polynomial Regression (Learner)	Numeric (multiple)	Scatter + graph of model
OSM Map View	Numeric (two)	Spatial data
OSM Map to Image	Numeric (two)	Spatial data, creates image
Hierarchical Cluster View	Distance and cluster model	Dendrogram

Node	Supported data types	Remarks
ROC Curve	Nominal and numeric (multiple)	
Enrichment Plotter	Numeric (multiple)	
Spark Line Appender	Numeric (multiple)	No view, but creates images
Radar Plot Appender	Numeric (multiple)	No view, but creates images

There are a few other view-related nodes in KNIME (and many more with mostly textual views). The **Image To Table** node can be useful when you want to iterate (loop) through certain parts generating images. Because the image ports (dark green filled rectangles) cannot be used with loop end nodes, you have to convert them to a table column. This is the exact purpose of the **Image To Table** node.

On the other hand, when you want an image port to hold an image (for example, to include it in a report), you should use the **Table To Image** node, which selects the first row's selected image column and returns it as an image port object.

The last notable node is the **Renderer to Image**. It simply grabs a column and the selected renderer, and creates an SVG or PNG image column with its content. You can use this later in web pages or other places, where supported. This is very handy when you want to handle a special kind of content; for example, molecules.

Visual guide for the views

In this section, we will introduce the iris dataset (*Frank, A. & Asuncion, A. (2010). UCI Machine Learning Repository* (http://archive.ics.uci.edu/ml). *Irvine, CA: University of California, School of Information and Computer Science.* Iris dataset: http://archive.ics.uci.edu/ml/datasets/Iris) with some screenshots from the views (without their controls).

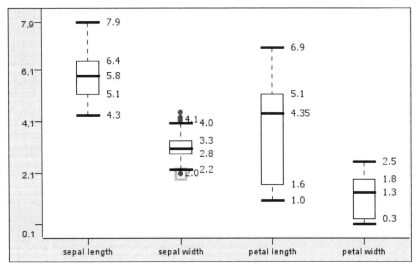

Box plot for the numeric columns

The **Conditional Box Plot** and the **Box Plot** nodes' views look similar. These are also sometimes called box-and-whisker diagrams. The **Box Plot** node visualizes the values of different columns, while the **Conditional Box Plot** view shows one column's values grouped by a nominal column's values. As you can see in the screenshot, the HiLite information is visible for the outliers (but only for those values). You can also select the outliers and HiLite them.

The shape of the outlier points is not influenced by the shape property.

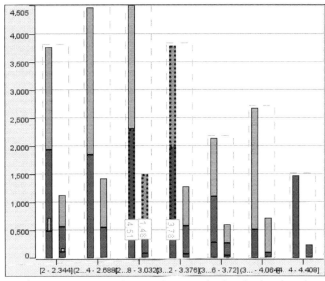

Histogram with a few columns selected, HiLited rows and colored values based on class attribute

As the screenshot shows, the **Histogram** node's view is capable of handling the color properties. It also supports the aggregation of different values, and the option to show the values for the selected (or all) columns. The adjacent columns within the dashed lines represent the different columns for each binning column value. This way, you can compare their distributions for certain aggregations. The interactive and the normal versions look quite similar, but they differ in configuration and view options.

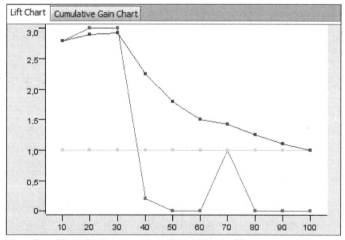

The Interactive Table view with changed renderer for petal length and color codes for class, Row43 is HiLited

The **Interactive Table** view first looks and works like a normal port view for a data table (such as the options on the context menu for the column header: **Available Renderers**, **Show Possible Values**, and sorting by *Ctrl* + clicking on the header; the latter can be done from the menu with a normal click, too), although it offers HiLiting and a few other options.

Lift chart of a model predicted by a decision tree, the colors are: red – lift, green – baseline, cumulative lift – blue

The **Lift Chart** view can help evaluate a models' performance. The **Cumulative Gain Chart** tab looks similar, although it has only two lines.

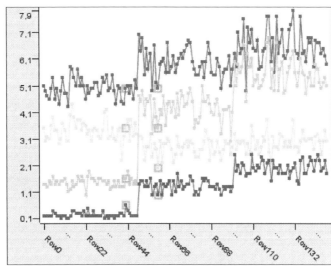

Line plot with some two HiLited rows and the four numeric columns: red – sepal length, yellowish – sepal width, green – petal length, blue – petal width

The **Line Plot** view can be used to compare the different columns of the same rows. The rows are along the x axis, while their values for different columns are along the y axis. The adjacent row's values for the same column are connected with a line.

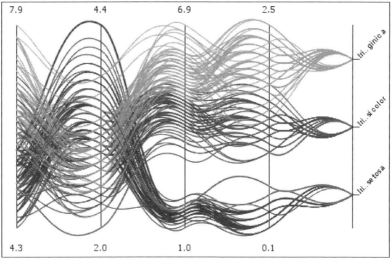

Parallel coordinates with colored curvy lines, the columns are: sepal length, sepal width, petal length, petal width and class

The **Parallel Coordinates** view can also visualize the individual rows, but in this case, the row values for the different columns are connected (with lines or with curves). In this case, the columns are along the x axis, while the values are along the y axis.

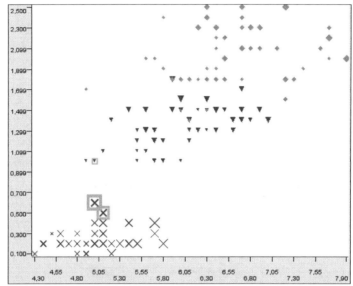

Scatterplot of sepal length vs. petal width with size information from sepal width

The **Scatter Plot** views can be used efficiently to visualize the two dimensions. Although, with the properties, the number of dimensions from which information is presented can grow to five.

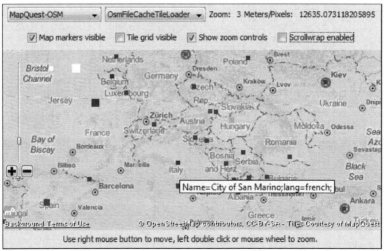

The Open Street Map integration offers many ways to visualize spatial data; it supports color, shape, and size properties and also works with HiLiting. Selected information from the input table is also available as a tooltip.

The **OSM Map View** and **OSM Map to Image** nodes are designed to show data on maps. They are very flexible, and can show many details, but they can also hide the distracting layers.

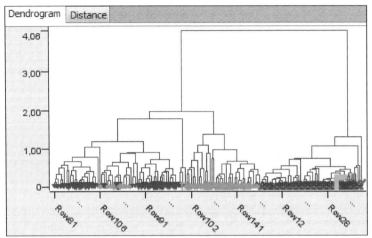

Hierarchical clustering dendrogram (average linkage with Euclidean distance using the numeric columns)

The best way to visualize a clustering is by using a dendrogram, because the distances between the clusters are visible in this way. The **Hierarchical Cluster** view offers this kind of model visualization. To show the similarity between the rows, first you have to compute the cluster model using the **Hierarchical Clustering (DistMatrix)** node from the KNIME Distance Matrix extension, available on the KNIME update site.

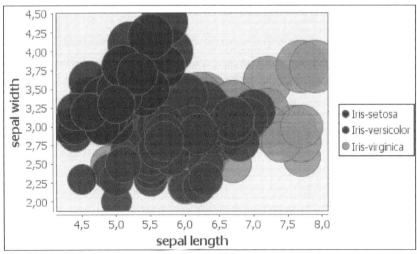

JFreeChart bubble chart

The **Bubble Chart (JFreeChart)** node can offer an alternative to the scatter plots; however, in this case, the dimension of the size is also mandatory.

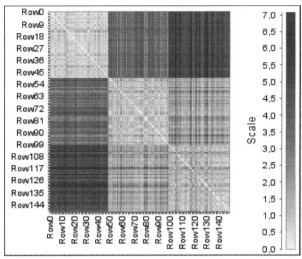

JFreeChart heatmap with Euclidean distance of numeric columns

The **HeatMap (JFreeChart)** node provides a way to visualize not just the collection columns, but also the distances, as shown in the previous screenshot. To use the regular tables, you might require a preprocessing step which uses the **Create Collection Column** or the **GroupBy** node to compute the distances, but it also works fine for displaying the values.

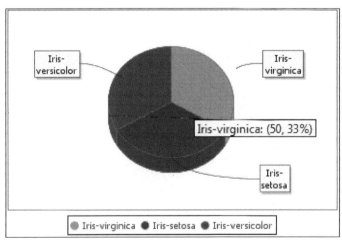

JFreeChart pie chart

The **Pie Chart (JFreeChart)** node also offers a visualization with a pie, and unlike the **Pie chart** and the **Pie chart (interactive)** nodes, this can create three-dimensional pies.

The spark lines and radar plot for numeric columns

The results of the **Spark Lines Appender** and the **Radar Plot Appender** nodes are not the individual views, but are the new columns with the SVG images generated for each row. We can use this in the next chapter.

Distance matrix

The distance matrix is used not just for visualization, but for learning algorithms too. You can think of them as a column of collections, where each cell contains the difference between the previous rows.

The supported distance functions are the following:

- Real distances
    - Euclidean($\|v_1 - v_2\|_2$)
    - Manhattan ($\|v_1 - v_2\|_1$)
    - Cosine ($1 - \frac{v_1 v_2}{\|v_1\|_2 \|v_2\|_2}$)
- Bitvector distances
    - Tanimoto ($1 - \frac{|v_1 v_2|}{|v_1| + |v_2| - |v_1 v_2|}$)
    - Dice ($1 - \frac{2|v_1 v_2|}{|v_1| + |v_2|}$)
    - Bitvector cosine ($1 - \frac{|v_1 v_2|}{|v_1| |v_2|}$)
- Distance vector (assuming you already have a distance vector, you can transform it to a distance matrix when there are row order changes or filtering)
- Molecule distances (from extensions)

The distance matrix feature can be used together with the hierarchical clustering, which also provides a node to view it; this is the main reason we introduced them in this chapter.

You can generate distances using the **Distance Matrix Calculate** node (just select the function, the numeric columns, and set the name. The chunk size is just for fine tuning larger tables), but you can also load that information with the **Distance Matrix Reader** node.The HiTS extension (http://code.google.com/p/hits) also provides a view to show dendrograms with heatmaps.

Using visual properties

One of KNIME's great features is that it allows you to set certain properties of the views in advance. So, you need not remember how you set them in one view and how it is set in another, you just have to connect them to the same table. This is a big step towards reproducible experimental results and figures with the ease of graphical configuration. Each property is applied to the rows based on column values, so changes in column values will affect (remove) the property and each kind of property is exclusive (a new node with the same kind of properties replaces the original property). When you want to reuse the properties in another place of the workflow, you can use the appender nodes.

The three supported properties are: color, size, and shape.

Color

With the **Color Manager** node, you can set the color for different rows. The colors can be assigned either to a nominal or a numeric column.

In the case of the nominal columns, each value can have a different color. This can be useful when you want to compare the actual or the predicted labels/classes of the rows.

When you assign colors to the numeric columns, the color of the minimal and the maximal value (as it is available in the column specification: **Lower Bound**, **Upper Bound**) should be specified. The remaining shades are linearly computed.

The **Color Appender** node allows you to use the same color configuration for other tables. Be careful when there are values outside the domain. The nearest extreme value is used in case of numeric columns and the black color is used for nominal columns. It is also possible to set an incompatible format to the column, but in that case, it will not be used.

Size

The size of the points can be really a good indicator of the nonvisible attributes. It allows you to have larger or smaller dots for the different data points in views. The size is computed by the **Size Manager** node as a function of the input from the minimal value to the maximal value, similar to the numeric color property. (Based on the domain bounds, outside them the nearest extreme is used.)

 Be careful not to use this node on columns where the minimum is less than zero (the logarithmic and the square root function would generate a complex number). Also, check the bounds after filtering; you might need to use the **Domain Calculator**.

The following are the supported functions:

- **LINEAR**: It is a linear function between the bounds
- **SQUARE_ROOT**: It is useful when you want a less increase in the higher values, but want more details of the lower values
- **LOGARITHMIC**: It is ideal when there is large difference between the bounds and more details near the lower bound is interesting
- **EXPONENTIAL**: The exponential function will make even small differences large

The **Size Appender** allows you to use the same size configurations in different places of the workflow, even for other columns.

Shape

The last property you can set is the shape of the points. For this purpose, you have the **Shape Manager** node, which allows you to set the shape based on a nominal column's values. Together with the **Color Manager,** you can visualize both the predicted and the original class of the training dataset. This can give you a better idea when the data is not properly learned and clustered, and might give you ideas to improve the settings.

Similar to other properties, the **Shape Appender** can bring the shape configuration to other parts of a workflow.

KNIME views

You can export the view contents to either the PNG or SVG files from the **File | Export as** menu. (The latter is only available when the KNIME SVG Support is installed.)

It is worth noting the other usual view controls. The **File** menu contains the **Always on top** and **Close** options, besides the previously discussed **Export as** menu. The first option allows you to compare the multiple views easily by having them side-by-side and still working with other windows.

The rest of the menus are related to HiLiting, which will be discussed soon.

The configuration of nodes usually includes an option of how many different values or how many rows should be used when you create the view. Because the views usually load all the data (or the specified amount) in the memory to have a resizable content, too many rows would require too much memory, while too many different values would make it hard to understand either the legends or the whole view in certain cases.

The mouse mode controls allow you to select certain points or set of points (for example, in the case of hierarchical clustering and the histogram nodes), to zoom in or to move around in a zoomed view. With the **Background Color** option, you can change the background of the plot. The **Use anti-aliasing** option can be used to apply subpixel rendering for fonts and lines.

HiLite

The **HiLite** menu consists of the **HiLite Selected, UnHiLite Selected**, and **Clear HiLite** items. With these items, you can create fine-grained HiLite rows. Once you select a few data points/rows, you can add or remove the HiLite signal using the first two options, and the third clears all the HiLite signals from this part of the workflow.

Lots of the nonview nodes also have HiLite-related options, which can be very handy when the row's IDs change and want to propagate HiLiting to the parts with different row IDs of the workflow; however, beware, as this usually requires additional memory.

The **Show/Hide** menu (or the **HiLite/Filter** menu) also helps the HiLite operations. The **Show hilited only** option hides all the non-HiLited rows/points. The default option is usually **Show all**, but the **Fade unhilited** option is a compromise between the two (shows both the kinds of data, but the non-HiLited are faded or grey).

Use cases for HiLite

You might wonder how this HiLite feature is useful.

With the **Box Plot** and the **Conditional Box Plot** nodes, you can select the rows that have extreme values in certain columns or extreme values within a class without creating complex filtering. (The extremity is defined as below $Q1 - 1.5IQR$ or as above $Q3 - 1.5IQR$

It is also useful to see the same selection of data from different perspectives. For example, you have the extremes selected based on some columns, but you are curious to know how they relate to other columns' values. The **Parallel Coordinates** or the **Line Plot** can give a visual overview of the values. The **Scatter Plot** (or the **Scatter Matrix**) node is also useful when different columns should be compared.

When you prefer the numeric/textual values of the selected rows, you should use the **Interactive Table** node. It allows you to check the HiLited and non-HiLited rows together or independently with the order of the column you want.

With the **Hierarchical Clustering View** node, you can select certain clusters (similar rows). This can also be useful to identify the outlier groups based on multiple columns (as the distances can be computed from more than one columns).

Row IDs

It is important to remember that the row IDs play an important role for most of the KNIME views. The row IDs are used as axis values; that is, tooltips. So, to create a nice, easy-to-understand figure/view, you have to provide as many useful row IDs as you can.

To use meaningful labels, you have to create a column with the proper (unique) values, and make that column a row ID with the help of the **RowID** node. This node also offers HiLite support (**Enable Hiliting**), so you do not have to make a compromise between neat figures and HiLiting.

Extreme values

The infinite values (`Double.POSITIVE_INFINITY` and `Double.NEGATIVE_INFINITY`) make the ranges meaningless, because these values are not measurable by normal real values.

The other special value is the `Double.NaN` (not a number) value, which you get, for example, when you divide zero by zero. It is not equal to any numeric value, not even to itself. It also makes comparison impossible, so it should be avoided as much as possible. The previous chapter has already introduced how to handle these cases.

The missing values are usually handled by not showing the rows containing them, but some views make it possible to use different strategies.

Basic KNIME views

The main views of KNIME give you multiple options to explore data. These nodes do not provide options to generate images for further nodes, but they give quite a good overview about the data, and you can save the files using the **File** menu.

There are different flavors for some of the nodes: the interactive and the normal. With the interactive flavor, you can modify certain parameters of the view without reconfiguring (and executing) the view. The interactive versions are better suited for data exploration, but the normal ones make it easier to check certain things with new data.

The Box plots

The **Box Plot** node has no configuration, but gives robust statistics (minimum, smallest, lower quartile, median, largest, and maximum) for numeric columns. You might wonder about the difference between the minimum and the smallest values or the largest and maximum values. The smallest is the maximum of the minimal value and the $Q1 - 1.5IQR = Q1 - 1.5(Q3 - Q1)$ value. The largest is computed analogously.

The view gives a box-and-whisker diagram, which is useful to find outliers. The **Column Selection** tab allows you to focus only on certain columns. The **Normalize** option on the **Appearance** tab will rescale the box-and-whisker diagrams to have the same length on the screen between the minimum and maximum values.

The **Conditional Box Plot** node's view is quite similar to the **Box Plot** view, although in this case, the diagram is not split by the columns, but by a preselected nominal column. The values are representing the values from a numeric column. You can also select whether the missing values should be visible or not.

The node view controls are really similar to the **Box Plot**'s. However, in this case, the **Column Selection** tab does not refer to the columns from the table, but to the columns on the diagram; you can select the class values that should be visible.

Hierarchical clustering

There is an option to visualize the result of hierarchical clustering with the **Hierarchical Cluster View** node; however, it is worth summarizing how you can reach the state when you can show the cluster model. First, you have to specify the distance between the rows using one of the options we described in the *Distance matrix* section.

In the **Hierarchical Clustering (DistMatrix)** node's configuration, the main option you have to select is the **Linkage Type**, which defines how the distance between the clusters should be measured:

- **Single**: It measures the minimal distance between the cluster points
- **Average**: It measures the average of differences between the points of the clusters
- **Complete**: It measures the maximal distance between the cluster points

You can also select between the distance matrices if you have multiple columns.

Histograms

The difference between **Histogram** and **Histogram (interactive)** is minimal in the configurations (the non-interactive version allows you to specify the number of bins configuration time). The common configuration options are the **Binning column**, **Aggregation column**, and the **No. of rows to display**. With the **Binning column** option, you can define how the main bins should be created; it can be either nominal or numeric. The coloring information splits between the bars, and the aggregation columns are available as separate, adjacent bars.

The possible aggregation options are: **Average**, **Sum**, **Row Count**, and **Row Count (w/o missing values)**. When you have multiple aggregation columns selected, **Row Count** (with missing values) is not an informative or recommended choice.

On the **Visualization settings** tab, you can further customize the view, by enabling/disabling outlines, grid lines, the orientation, width, or the labels.

The **Details** tab gives the information about the selected bars, such as the average, sum, count for each column, and colors. (You can select the monochrome part of a bar too.)

Interactive Table

The interactive table looks like a plain port view; however, it gives further options, such as the HiLiting support and the optional color information (in the port view, it is not optional). You can also save the content to the CSV file (**Output | Write CSV**), adjust the default column and row size (**View | Row Height... and Column Width...**), and find certain values (**Navigation | Find**, *Ctrl + F*).

The options for sorting by columns (*Ctrl* + click, or the menu from the regular click) and reordering (dragging) them are also available in this view, and you can select the preferred renderers for them. However, you cannot check the metadata information (column stats and the properties).

The Lift chart

The **Lift Chart** node is useful when you want to evaluate the fit of a model for a binominal class. In the configuration dialog, you can specify what is the training label and the value learned. The probabilities of the learned label should also be specified, just like the width of the bins (in percentage, you will get 100/that value points). In the view, there are two parts—**Lift Chart** and **Cumulative Chart**—both with separate configurations of color, line widths and dot sizes (with visibilities).

The **Lift Chart** node also contains the cumulative lift, but it can be made invisible if you do not want it.

Lines

The **Line Plot** node and the **Parallel Coordinates** views are similar, but they show the data in the orthogonal/transposed form with respect to each other. The **Parallel Coordinates** view contains the selected columns on the x axis and the row values flow horizontally colored by the color properties, while in **Line Plot**, the rows are on the x axis and the (numeric) columns are represented by user-defined colors.

The missing values are handled differently; in **Line Plot**, you can try to interpolate, while in the other, you can either omit or show them or their rows.

Line Plot is more suited for equidistant data, such as time series, for other data it might give misleading results (the distances between the rows are the same). The **Parallel Coordinates** view is better suited to find connections between the values of different columns, because in this case you have no ordering bias. The **Parallel Coordinates** view gives a neat option to use curves instead of straight lines. Fortunately, you can change the order of columns within the view using the extra mouse mode **Transformation**, so you can create neat figures with this view. This view is quite good to show intuitive correlations.

Pie charts

The **Pie Chart** and the **Pie Chart (interactive)** nodes have the same configuration options, although for the latter, the configuration gives only the overridable defaults in the view. These configurations include the binning column and the aggregation column, just like the aggregation function.

With *Ctrl* + click, you can select multiple pies. HiLiting works in this view, and the **Details** tab contains statistical information for each selected sections, which is split by the colors within the pies. When the binning is not consistent with the color property, no coloring is applied unless you select them (and enable the **Color selected** section).

In the **Visualization setting** tab, you can specify whether the section representing the missing values should be visible or not, show outline, explode the selection, or whether the aggregated value/percent should be visible or not (for selected, all, or no sections). The size of the diagram too can be adjusted in this tab.

The Scatter plots

The **Scatter Matrix** and the **Scatter Plot** nodes are quite similar. The **Scatter Matrix** node is a generalization of the latter. It allows you to check the scatter plots for different columns side-by-side.

A scatter plot can use all the visual properties (size, shape, and color), so you can visualize up to five different columns' values on a 2D plot.

There are not many configurations for either maximum rows or maximum distinct nominal values in a column.

In the case of **Scatter Plot**, you can only select the two columns for the x and y axes, but in case of the **Scatter Matrix** node, you can set the ranges for them. With the **Scatter Matrix,** you can select multiple columns, and when you are in the **Transformation mouse** mode, you can rearrange the rows/columns, but you cannot change their ranges.

Both the views support the jittering when one of the columns is nominal (the **Appearance** tab, **Jitter slider**). In that case, the values in the other dimension get some random noise, so the number of points at a position could be easily estimated. If you want precise positions, you might consider adding transparency to the color of the points, so when there are overlaps, they will be more visible.

The **Linear Regression (Learner)** and the **Polynomial Regression (Learner)** nodes also provide the scatter plot views, although these show the model as a line. It can be useful to have a visual view of the regression, even though these do not specify which slice of the function is shown from the many possible functions, parallel to the selected.

Spark Line Appender

The **Spark Line Appender** node does not have a view, but it generates a column with an SVG image of a line plot of the selected numeric columns, for that row. This can be useful to find interesting patterns. However, it is recommended to use **Interactive Table**, because the initial size is hard to see, and changing the row height multiple times is not so much fun (and can be avoided if you hold the *Shift* key while you resize the height of a row). But with the special view, you can do that from the menu.

Radar Plot Appender

The **Radar Plot Appender** node works quite like the previous node, although it has more configuration options. You can set many colors for the SVG cell, and also the ranges and the branches (columns) of the radar plot. The resulting table has a bit larger predefined row height, but the use of an **Interactive Table** view might still be a good idea.

The Scorer views

The **ROC Curve (ROC (Receiver Operating Characteristic))** and **Enrichment Plotter** nodes give options to evaluate a certain model's performance visually. Because the views are not too interactive, you have to specify every parameter upfront in the configuration dialog.

In the **ROC Curve** configuration, you have to select the binominal **Class column** and the label (**Positive class value**) to which the probabilities belong. This way, you will be able to compare different kinds of models or models with different parameters. The node also provides the areas beneath the ROC curve in the result table.

The **Enrichment Plotter** node helps you decide where to set the cut-off point to select the hits. The node description gives a more detailed guide on how to use it.

JFreeChart

The **JFreeChart** nodes are not installed by default, but the extension is available from the standard KNIME update site under the name **KNIME JFreeChart**.

The common part of these nodes is that you have to specify the appearance of the result in advance, and the focus is not on the view, but on the resulting image port object.

In the **General Plot Options Configuration** tab, you can specify the type of the resulting image (PNG or SVG), the size, the title, colors, and the font size (relative to the standard font for each item printed).

You can use the port objects in the reports, but you can also use them to check certain properties if you iterate through a loop and convert the result with **Image To Table**.

It is important to note that the customizable **JFreeChart View** tab is only available in freshly executed nodes. The generated image can be visualized either using the view or the image output.

In the **JFreeChart View** tab, you can customize (from the context menu) almost every aspect of the diagram (fonts, colors, tics, ranges, orientation, and outline style). This way, the output can be of quite a high quality. It is also important to note that the export is easier: you can use the **Copy** option to copy it to the clipboard or directly use the **Save as...** option to save it as a PNG file, and because there are no visible controls, you do not have to cut them off.

These nodes do not support HiLiting, but they provide tooltips about values. The support for properties is usually not implemented.

You can zoom in on these nodes by selecting a region (left to right, top to bottom) and zoom out by selecting in the opposite direction. You can also use the context menu's zooming options. (It seems that you cannot move around using the mouse or keyboard, so you have to zoom out and select another region if you want to see the details of that region.)

The Bar charts

The **Bar Chart (JFreeChart)** node's view is similar to a usual histogram, but it does not allow any other aggregation other than the count function, and only nominal columns are accepted. The color of the first column can be specified, just like the labels for the axis. The nominal columns' values can be rotated, and the angle can be set. You can also enable/disable the legends.

The **GroupBy Bar Chart (JFreeChart)** node's configuration is similar, except in this case, the nominal column is a single column (it can also be numeric), and the rest of the numeric columns can be visualized against it. It is important to note that the binning column should contain unique values. (The numeric values are grouped by these values.)

The Bubble chart

The **Bubble Chart (JFreeChart)** node's view is analogous to the **Scatter Plot** view, but in this case, you cannot set the color and the shape, but the color is not opaque. It also cannot handle nominal columns, so you have to convert them to numbers if you want to plot them against other columns. You must specify the x and y positions of the bubbles, just like their radius.

Heatmap

The **Heatmap (JFreeChart)** node is capable of visualizing not just the values in multiple columns, but also the distances from the other color-coded rows, when a distance column is available.

The extreme colors can be specified in the **HeatMap (JFreeChart)** node's configuration for the minimal and the maximal distance, and the legend can also be visible or hidden. The labels for the axes can be specified, and the tooltip is also available on demand.

The Histogram chart

This is a bit different from the histogram views previously introduced. In this view, the histograms can be either behind or in front of other histograms. The different ranges are shown on the same scale, so some of them can be wider while the others are narrower.

The color of the bars is only adjustable for the first column. The histograms are plotted in order, the last is at the back, while the first is in the front. You cannot change the order of the histograms from the view of **Histogram (JFreeChart)**.

The Interval chart

The **Interval Chart (JFreeChart)** node's view is not so interesting when your label is not unique (or the order is not defined by its alphabetical order). But this view supports the time values without the need to transform your data with time information before visualization, focusing on that information.

You can specify the grouping nominal column (**Label**) and the start and end positions of the time intervals. Each row represents an interval.

It supports the color properties, so you can create overlapping intervals with different colors.

The Line chart

The **Line Chart (JFreeChart)** node's view is quite similar to the regular **Line Plot** view, except in this case, you cannot have dots to show the values. However, there is an extra input table to specify the colors of the series.

The other difference is that when specified, you can use the numeric or date column's values instead of the rows for the values of other columns; however, the connections are still done by the adjacent rows.

The Pie chart

The **Pie Chart (JFreeChart)** node's view is similar to the **Pie Chart** node, but it is less interactive. It still uses the color properties (as opposed to the other JFreeChart nodes) and can draw the pie in 3D.

The Scatter plot

The **Scatter Plot (JFreeChart)** node uses the shape and color properties, so it can visualize at most four columns. This is still quite static but configurable, and the result looks good (it can contain the legend, so it is practically ready to paste).

This node is quite constant too; you have to decide which columns should be there in the configuration dialog.

Open Street Map

In the **KNIME Labs Extensions** (available from the main KNIME update site) you can install the **KNIME Open Street Map Integration** in order to visualize spatial data.

This extension contains two nodes, **OSM Map View** and **OSM Map to Image**. The first one is the interactive, you can browse the map and check the data points (the tooltips can give details about them), think find the distribution of interesting points by HiLiting them. (HiLiting cannot be done using these nodes, but you can select area "blindly" if you use a **Scatter Plot** with the longitude and latitude information.)

Both nodes require coordinates to be in the range of -90 to 90 for latitude and -180 to 180 for longitude if there is an input table (which is optional). The image node's configuration includes a map to select which area should be visible on the resulting image, the configuration for the coordinates is on the **Map Marker** tab.

In the **OSM Map View**, you can browse by holding the right mouse button down and moving around. Zooming is configured for double-click and mouse wheel.

3D Scatterplot

We are highlighting a view from the many third party views because this is really neatly done, and you might not find it initially interesting if you do not work with chemical data.

In the **Erl Wood Open Source Nodes** extension (from the community update site), you can find a node called **2D/3D Scatterplot**. It allows you to plot 3D data and still use KNIME The HiLite functionality and the color, and size properties (but that can also be selected on demand). This is a very well designed and implemented view node. Its configuration is limited to column filtering and the number of rows/distinct values that should be on the screen.

This node does not support the automatic generation of a diagram. It's more focused towards exploration and not towards creating final figures.

It can also provide a regression fit line in 2D mode. It can be a good alternative to the normal **Scatter Plot** node too (unless you need the shape properties).

A right-click on the canvas gives information about the nearest point as a tooltip, which can be very useful when you need more information about the other dimensions (even the chemical structures and images are rendered nicely).

In the 3D mode, you can select points while holding down the *Ctrl* key.

Other visualization nodes

There are many options to show data, and you really do not have to limit yourself with those which are bundled with KNIME. In the community contributions (http://tech.knime.org/community), there are many options available. We will cherry-pick some of the more general and interesting visualization nodes.

The R plot, Python plot, and Matlab plot

The R plot, Python plot, and Matlab plot are available from the corresponding scripting extensions (the **KNIME R Scripting** extension, **KNIME Python Scripting** extension, and **KNIME Matlab Scripting** extension) on the community nodes update site.

The usage of these nodes do not require experience in the corresponding programming languages. There are templates from which you can choose and the parameters can be adjusted using KNIME controls. Obviously, you can create your own templates or fine-tune existing ones if you are not satisfied.

You need to have access to (possibly local) servers to connect to the extensions. (The **Python Plot** node uses (C)Python with some extensions.)

These nodes also generate images as their outputs in the PNG format.

Please take a look at their figure template gallery (`http://idisk-srv1.mpi-cbg.de/knime/scripting-templates_public/figure-template-gallery.html`) to get an idea of what is possible and how they look.

The official R plots

The **KNIME R Statistics Integration** extension from the main KNIME update site offers similar options like the **R Plot** discussed previously, but it does require some R programming knowledge (the templates help the configuration).

When you want to use it locally, you will need the **Table R-View** node, but when you use an R server, you should use the **R View (Remote)** node. The result is also available in the PNG format.

The recently introduced **R View** and other interactive KNIME nodes offer other options for the visualization of data. For details, please check KNIME's site at `http://tech.knime.org/whats-new-in-knime-28`

The RapidMiner view

The **RapidMiner Viewer** node is available on the community nodes and offers the **Plot View** and the **Advanced Charts** modes to visualize the data using RapidMiner's results view. It requires some pre-configuration, but after that, you will have a powerful tool for visual data exploration. (Unfortunately, it does not use many KNIME features; it neither supports HiLiting, color, shape, or size properties, nor provides the figure as an image.)

The views offer a wide range of visualization options and give highly customizable figures. It can even de-pivot in the view, so you do not have to create complex workflows to get an overview of the data. This view supports the following plots: Scatter, Scatter Multiple, Scatter Matrix, Scatter 3D, Scatter 3D Color, Bubble, Parallel, Deviation, Series, Series Multiple, Survey, SOM, Block, Density, Pie, Pie 3D, Ring, Bars, Bars Stacked, Pareto, Andrews Curves, Distribution, Histogram, Histogram Color, Quartile, Quartile Color, Quartile Color Matrix, Sticks, Sticks 3D, Box, Box 3D, and Surface 3D.

The Advanced Charts also support multiple visualizations. You can set the color, shape, and the size dimensions, although these are not auto-populated by the available properties. With the Advanced Charts, the details of the diagram can be configured in more depth than with the **JFreeChart**. It is worth reading the user manual of RapidMiner in this regard at `http://docs.rapid-i.com/files/rapidminer/RapidMiner-5.2-Advanced-Charts-english-v1.0.pdf`.

This node allows you to export the figure (without the controls) in various image formats. It is available from the icon in the upper-right corner.

The HiTS visualization

The HiTS visualization might not fit the previous extensions as it is not available on the usual KNIME update sites. But it might bring your attention to look for alternative options when you need a functionality, because there are many KNIME nodes available besides the one we saw in the previous sections.

The HiTS extension's website is `https://code.google.com/p/hits/`. The update site is `http://hits.googlecode.com/svn/trunk/ie.tcd.imm.hits.update/`. On the website, look for the **HiTS experimental features** (and also check its dependencies: HiTS main feature and HiTS third party components feature) in the HiTS main category.

The **Plate Heatmap** node might not be so interesting, because it is quite specific to high content/throughput screening, but the **Simple Heatmap** and the **Dendrogram with Heatmap** nodes are generally useful. These support the HiLite feature and give an overview about the data with color codes.

The **Dendrogram with Heatmap** node uses the hierarchical clustering model to show the dendrogram. Together with the heatmap, it gives you a better idea about your clusters.

Tips for HiLiting

HiLiting gives great tools for various tasks: outlier detection, manual row selection, and visualization of a custom subset.

Using Interactive HiLite Collector

First, let's assume you want to label the different outlier categories. In case of an iris dataset, the outlier categories should be the high sepal length, high sepal width, high petal length, high petal width, and their lower counterparts. You can also select the outliers by different classes (iris-setosa, iris-versicolor, and iris-virginica) for each column (in both extreme directions), which gives $4 \cdot 3 \cdot 2 = 24$ possible options. Quite a lot, but you will need only four views to compute these (and only a single, if you do not want to split according to the classes).

Let's see how this can be done. We will cover only the simpler (no-class) analysis.

Connect the **Box Plot** node to the data source. Also, connect the **Interactive HiLite Collector** node to it. Open both the views; you should execute **Box Plot**, and the collector.

There are only four outlier points on this plot: three high values for sepal width and one low value also for sepal width. First, you can select and HiLite, for example, the high values. Now switch to the collector view and set a label to this group (for example, high sepal width), and also check the **New Column** checkbox. Once done, click on **Apply**. Now you can clear the HiLite (from any view) and select the other group and HiLite. Go to the collector again and give a name to this group too; then click on **Apply** again (keeping the **New Column** option on).

The **Interactive HiLite Collector** node is executed by every click on **Apply** and augment the original table with two new columns. The different labels are in the new columns. The rows that are not marked contain missing values in those columns.

If you do not check the **New Column** checkbox (when you click on **Apply**), the values will go to the same column. If there were already some value(s), then the new value will be appended, separated by a comma (,).

You can start a new selection after you reset the **Interactive HiLite Collector** node, but you can use a different collector if you want to keep the previous selection.

In the final result, you might want to replace the missing values with something, such as the text `normal` using the **Missing Value** node. (Do not forget to recalculate the domain with the **Domain Calculator** node for certain use cases.) This way, you can further visualize, add color, or shape properties. With this information, you can have better understanding and can find other connections among the data.

When you need only a single HiLited/non-HiLited option to split the data, you should use the **HiLite Filter** option (yes, it would be more consistent if it were named HiLite Splitter, but for historical reasons, this name remained).

Finding connections

We already mentioned the tip to further process the result of the **Interactive HiLite Collector** node. That way, you can identify various outliers and compare them to other dimensions; for example, with **Parallel Coordinates**, **Line Chart**, or one of the scatter plots.

 Use **Color Manager** or **Shape Manager** to change the plot of the points.

Most of the nodes supporting HiLite also support filtering out the non-HiLited rows; because you can have multiple views open, and also focus only on the interesting rows/points in the other views too.

When you pivot or group according to the table, you can still use HiLiting, so you can select an interesting point in one table and HiLite it; on the other end, the corresponding rows will also be HiLited. For example, with this technique you can use **Box Plot** instead of the **Conditional Box Plot,** and you do not need to iterate through the possible columns individually.

Visualizing models

In the previous chapter, we created a workflow to generate a grid. That must have looked pointless at that time, but now, we will move a bit forward and show an application. The `GenerateGridForLogisticRegression.zip` file contains the workflow demonstrating this idea with the iris dataset.

In this workflow, we use a setup very similar to the **Generate Grid** workflow till the preprocessing meta node, but in this case, we use the average of minimum and maximum values instead of creating NaN values when we generate a grid with a single value in that dimension. (This will be important when we apply the model.) We also modified the grid parameters to be compatible with the iris dataset. In the lower region of the workflow, we load the iris dataset from `http://archive.ics.uci.edu/ml/datasets/Iris`, so we can create a logistic regression model with the **Logistic Regression (Learner)** node (it uses all numeric columns).

We would like to apply this model to both the data and the grid. This is an easy part; we can use two **Logistic Regression (Predictor)** nodes.

Exercise

Once you understand the details of the **Prepare** (combine) meta node, try to modify the workflow to use a single predictor. (You can use the **Row Filter** node for an efficient solution, but other options are also possible.)

Let's see what is inside the **Prepare (combine)** meta node. It uses three input tables: the configuration, the grid, and the data. We use the configuration to iterate through the other tables' content and bin them according to the configuration settings.

There is one problem though. When you select a single point for one of the dimensions, the grid will only have that value for binning, and the data values will not be properly binned. For this reason, we will add the data to create a single bin. But when the minimum and maximum values are present, we do not include them because that would cause different bin boundaries. To express this condition, we use two **Java IF (Table)** nodes and an **End IF** node.

With the **Auto-Binner** node, we create the bins. We have to keep only the newly created binned column (**Auto-Binner (Apply)**). So, we first have to compute its name (**add [Binner] Java Edit Variable**), then set as include column filter.

Finally, we collect the new columns (the **Loop End (Column Append)** node's "**Loop has same row IDs in each iteration**" option) and join the two old (data and grid) tables with the new bin columns using the **Joiner** node.

You might wonder why we have to bin the values at all. Look at the following figure:

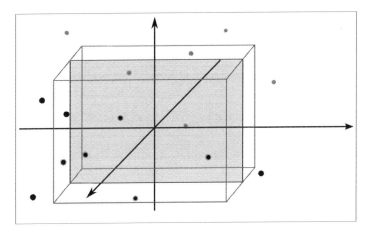

In the three-dimensional space, we have some points and a plane orthogonal to one of the axes; on that plane, there is a single red point. On most of the planes there are no points; the circled points are between the two blue planes

If we would slice by a single value on the orthogonal axis, there would be no values most of the time. For this reason, we select a region (a bin on the orthogonal axis) where we assume that the points would behave similarly when we project them to the plane we selected. (That is the cuboid in the figure; however, that is not limited to the non-orthogonal axis.)

Alright; so, we have these projections, but the points can be in multiple projections. We have to select only a single one to not get confused. To achieve this, we have added two **Nominal Value Row Filters** (filter by bin one and filter by bin two). (In the current initial configuration, this is not required, but it is usually necessary.)

How many Row Filters do we need in the general case?

The number of columns used to generate the model specifies the number of dimensions visualized in the view (for example, if we add a size manager we would need only a single row filter).

Now, we add the training class information (class column) as a shape property (the grid does not have this information) with the **Shape Manager** and add the predicted class (class (prediction) column) as colors with the **Color Manager**.

Finally, we add the **Scatter Plot** node to visualize the data.

Exercise

Can you generate all the possible slices for the grid? (You should increase the current 1 grid parameters before doing this.) With the **Scatter Plot (JFreeChart)** node, you can generate quite similar figures.

KNIME has many nodes, not just for visualization, but for classification too. This gives the idea for the next exercise.

Exercise

Try other classification models and check how they look like compared to the logistic regression. Try other visualizing options too.

Further ideas

One of our problems was that we cannot visualize four dimensions of data (with two dimensions of nominal information) on the screen. Could we use a different approach to approximate this problem? (Previously, we created slices of the space, projected to 2D planes, and visualized the plane.) We are already familiar with the dimension reduction techniques from the previous chapter. Why not use them in this visualization task? We can do that. And it might be interesting to see which one is easier to understand.

Where should we put the MDS or PCA transformation? It has to be somewhere between the data and the visualization. But, should it be before the model learning or after that? Both have advantages. When you reduce the dimensions after model learning, you are creating the model with more available information, so it might get better results and you can use that model without dimension reduction too. On the other hand, when you do the dimension reduction in advance, the resulting model is expressed in the reduced space. It can be simpler, even more accurate (because the dimension reduction could rotate and transform the data to an easier-to-learn form), and faster.

Exercise
Try the different dimension reduction techniques before and after learning. Also try different classification tasks too. Does one of them give you neat figures?

It might be interesting to see the transformed grid too, because the different dimension reduction techniques will give different results. These will give some clue about where the original points were. HiLiting is a great tool to understand these transformations.

Exercise
In your data analysis practice, you could try to adapt one of the techniques we introduced. In real-world data, different approaches might work better.

Summary

In this chapter, we introduced the main visualization nodes and the statistical techniques that could be used to explore your data. We built on the knowledge you gathered in the previous chapter, because data transformation is inevitable in a complex analysis. The HiLiting was previously introduced, but with the use cases in this chapter, you might now have a better idea about when you should use it.

4
Reporting

In this chapter, we will demonstrate how to create nicely formatted documents from the data you gathered, with KNIME's report designer. To achieve this, we introduce some new concepts specific to the reporting extension, and show how to use the report designer to create templates and reports. In this chapter, we'll cover the following topics:

- Reporting concepts
- Importing data
- Using the designer
- Generate the report document
- KNIME integration-specific topics

Installation of the reporting extensions

The standard KNIME desktop distribution does not contain reporting capabilities, but **KNIME Report Designer** and **KNIME HTML/PDF Writer** extensions are available from the standard KNIME update site to generate reports. The latter is optional and not covered in this book.

This is not distributed under the standard KNIME open source license (based on GNU GPL). It is still free, but in this case you are not allowed to modify the master page of the report template.

We will cover the report designer in detail. KNIME uses **Eclipse BIRT (Business Intelligence and Reporting Tools)** to design and generate reports. Eclipse BIRT has a large community, providing a lot of products and tools. You can check it on the eclipse marketplace at `http://marketplace.eclipse.org/category/categories/birt`. The Eclipse version for KNIME 2.8.x is 3.7.2, so you might want to filter accordingly. The marketplace client for Eclipse 3.7 is available from the main eclipse update site at `http://download.eclipse.org/releases/indigo/` with updates at `http://download.eclipse.org/eclipse/updates/3.7`. This way you can be sure you will install only compatible extensions, although there is always a chance that the feature you install will not be available readily.

These extensions include additional report items (bar codes, charts, and so on), functions, data sources, but also new export formats (RTF, DOCX, XLSX, and so on). You can also create your own if you need your functionality to be unique.

Reporting concepts

In this section, we will introduce the main concepts related to reports.

First of all, what is a **report**? It is a formatted document. It can include figures, text, and tables, possibly in a highly customized way.

The report is generated from a **report design** and some data. The report design is created from a *template*; it consists of a *layout* and a *master page*. The master page and the layout are similar in function; however, the master page is only for the header and footer of the pages, and the layout provides the main/body content.

The data can be from various data sources, for example, cubes, databases, and others; for now, we are focusing on KNIME data that is imported using the special nodes. The data imported is named a **data set**.

The **data cube** is a multidimensional data set, which can be used to summarize other data sets. You can think of it as a more processed, derived data set.

The reports can have **report parameters** and **report variables**, which can be further processed with (JavaScript) **scripts**.

There are special **functions** which help in transforming and processing the data. You can also find more implementations of other functions, so it is worth checking the Internet if you need to do something that is not supported by the default installation. You can use these functions in the scripts, although most of the tasks can be done in KNIME in advance.

The **report items** are the building blocks of the layout and the master page. There are various options to generate report items. You can also design your own report items if you miss one; however, chances are high that there already are solutions for that purpose, so you just have to select the best for your tasks.

AutoTexts and **QuickTools** both add more options in report design. QuickTools are only available for layout, but AutoTexts are only available for the master page.

The **resources** of a report are usually static images and scripts. They are often copied to the workflow's folder and referenced from there.

The **report designer** perspective can be used to create and customize the report design.

Document/report **emitters** can generate a report in various formats. Different emitters are available for most of the common formats, and you can write your own if you want. The report generation is done in three phases: **preparation**, **generation**, and **presentation**. For more details, you will find a nice figure describing the generation from the scripting perspective on the page: `http://www.eclipse.org/birt/phoenix/deploy/reportScripting.php`

The **styles** and **themes** can be used to have the report look consistent, so you can have a result that fits well to other parts of your resources. For details, you can check the page `http://www.packtpub.com/article/creating-themes-report-birt` that has an article from *John Ward*. You can apply styles to individual items, while the themes contain the default styles for the items.

Importing data

There are many options to import data to a report. For example, you can use SQL databases and access them through JDBC; however, you can also use this feature to import KNIME nodes' exported tabular content with a proper JDBC driver, although this is not the recommended way.

The **Data** menu can be used to create a new data set, data cube, or data source.

Sending data and images to a report

The first thing you might notice after the install is that you have a new category named **Reporting** with two new nodes within **Node Repository**. The **Data to Report** node brings a table to the report as a data source and creates a data set for it.

There are not many configuration options here; one is where you can set how images within the table should be handled. For example, an image can be resized to a fixed size. Here, ideally the best option would be to use SVG, although using SVG is a bit harder. The node description gives a detailed description on how to use them; however, unfortunately, the preview does not support the rendering of SVG images, so you will need to generate them to check for the results.

In reporting, the combination of different tables is a bit more limited, so it might be necessary to combine the tables to a denormalized table too.

The date and time data columns are imported as strings, so in the designer, you will need to change that to Date, Date Time, or Time. When the data is an image, it is not automatically represented as an image. It is imported as a blob that stands for a large binary object. You need to use report items for those supporting images.

Dates

Because the dates are imported as a string, you have to create a computed column if you prefer to use them as a date. For cubes, this is a strongly recommended transformation to do.

The **Image to Report** node acts similar to the **Data to Report** node, although it makes only a single image available in the report designer from an image port object.

The preferences for the **Image to Report** node are similar to the **Data to Report** node's preferences and works in the same way.

Importing from other sources

When it comes to data presentation, you might want to enrich the data from another source to make it more up-to-date, or just import a table structure file already processed with KNIME or exported from KNIME.

There are multiple **ODA (Open Data Access)** data source importer extensions available for BIRT. So, besides the default options, you can import from other reports or different services.

Check the BIRT exchange marketplace at http://www.birt-exchange.com/be/marketplace/app-listing/ for the BIRT emitter or ODA extensions besides the BIRT-related section of the eclipse marketplace at http://marketplace.eclipse.org/category/categories/birt.

The default data providers include: the flat file, JDBC, KNIME, scripted, and XML source support.

To import a new data source, you have to open a view showing the **Data Explorer** or the **Outline** view. Then, you can select the **New Data Source** option from the context menu.

From the data source, you can create data sets; using the context menu of **Data Sets**, select the **New Data Set** menu item.

With flat files, you can import files separated by a comma (**CSV**), space (**SSV**), tab (**TSV**), or pipe (|, **PSV** (pipe separated values)). When the type of the columns is specified in the second row, it can parse the input accordingly. You can import data locally or from a URI.

With the **JDBC Data Source**, you have to specify the connection settings, and then you can use that data source to import tables, such as data sets. You can also bind the connection settings or use a connection profile store. An example data source is also available; you can check the BIRT tutorial about its usage at:

```
http://www.eclipse.org/birt/phoenix/tutorial/basic/basic04.php
```

You cannot add another **KNIME Data Source**, although one is enough to get multiple tables imported. Therefore, it is not necessary either.

With a **Scripted Data Source**, you can compute and import data using JavaScript; for example, using RESTful services with JSON results are well suited for this kind of data source.

The **XML Data Source** can be used to import XML files with a schema. The schema is optional, although useful to have. In the associated data sets, you can define the columns using XPath expressions.

Joining data sets

When you have multiple but possibly semantically connected data sets, you might want to connect them. You just need to create a new data set by selecting the **New Joint Data Set** menu item from the context menu of **Data Sets**.

There you have to select the columns you want to join, and the way you want to connect them: **Inner Join**, **Left Outer Join**, **Right Outer Join**, and **Full Outer Join**. After that you will be asked to set further options, such as the output or computed columns, the parameters of the data set, and the possible filters. You also have an option to preview the resulting data set.

Preferences

After you have installed the plugin, a few new options will appear in **File | Preferences**.

The two main parts of the new options are **KNIME | Report Designer** and **Report Design**. In **KNIME | Report Designer** there are only two options, which you most probably do not want to change if you prefer having an up-to-date state of the data.

In **Report Design**, there are many preferences; we will cover only a subset of them.

Within **Report Design**, the **Preview** subpage might be interesting, because you can customize how the preview should work, such as setting the locale, time zone, bidirectional orientation, using external browser, or enabling SVG charts. You can also disable the master page in previews. In its **Data** subpage, you can set bounds on data usage for previews. If you are bound by your machine running KNIME, you can also use a server to generate the preview of the reports. To do this, you have to specify the server in the **Preview Server** page in **Report Design**.

In **Report Design | Crosstab**, **Chart**, and **Data Set Editor**, you can also set limits on the data to show/use and affect the behavior of the editors.

The report templates and the report resource folders can be set in **Report Design | Template** and **Resource** respectively.

In **Report Design | Layout**, you can specify the units (**Auto**, **in**, **cm**, **mm**, **points**, or **picas**) that you want to see/use in the report design.

By default, you can only use **JavaScript Syntax** for expressions (**Report Design | Expression Syntax**), and that is the recommended one , because script generators and templates usually use JavaScript.

In **Report Design | Comment Template**, you can specify whether a template should be used for new files, and what it should be.

In the preference page, you can see a link named **Configure Project Specific Settings...**, although the KNIME workflows are not compatible with the expected reporting projects. Therefore, you cannot select any workflows/reports available from KNIME.

Using the designer

There is a good introduction to BIRT at `http://www.eclipse.org/birt/phoenix/tutorial/`—although the KNIME version is slightly different, it still offers information on few other options. Some of the views are not visible by default, so we will explain how you can create report designs for your workflow.

You might realize that when you installed the reporting extension, a new button appeared on the toolbar. The icon looks like four yellow/orange stripes and a line plot with four points. Also, it is on the right-hand side of the zooming factor. When you have saved your workflow, click it and apply the changes, so that the data from KNIME will be available as a data set.

Then, you open the KNIME report designer perspective, and you should get a dialog about the new data being available. It is recommended to apply the changes so that you will get the updated data in the designer, the preview, and in the reports.

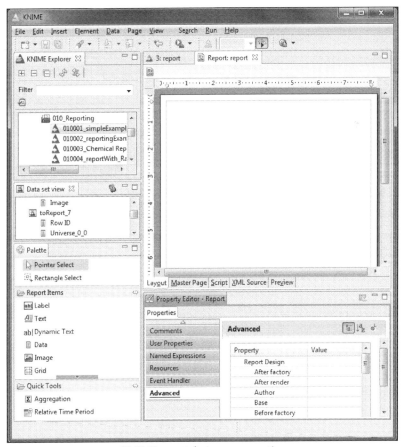

KNIME report designer perspective

You can immediately see that this is quite different from the normal KNIME perspective, although there are familiar views, such as **KNIME Explorer**; also, the toolbar contains the buttons that were discussed previously.

The **KNIME Explorer** view can be safely closed or minimized to quick views, or hidden as a sibling tab, because opening a workflow from it will leave the reporting perspective. You can also leave and go back to the workflow belonging to the report using the button with the KNIME symbol or by selecting the workflow tab in the editor area.

On the toolbar, you can find two more buttons; one of them toggles between the breadcrumb path of the actual element, while the other opens the report in the report viewer (or in the external browser of your choice). From the latter's menu, you can select the generation of the report in a different format too.

There is a view named **Data set view**, which allows you to check the contents of the tables you imported and synchronize the content of the view with the associated workflow—if there was a change and was not applied, you can apply that change any time. The report parameters are also available in this view.

The **Palette** view is similar to **Node Repository** in the basic KNIME perspective; however, here you are not selecting nodes, but report items, and quick tools are available (and you can specify the mouse selection behavior). Similarly, you can grab an item from the **Palette** and place it on the editor area. When you edit master pages, quick tools will be replaced with auto-text items.

The **Property Editor** view is an important part of the perspective, where you can adjust and change the properties of the selected item. These properties are arranged in categories, making it easier to find the appropriate one.

The **Report** editor has five tabs: **Layout**, **Master Page**, **Script**, **XML Source**, and **Preview**. You can also use the **Page** menu to switch between the tabs.

The **Layout** tab is usually used most often when you want to edit. It is almost like a what-you-see-is-what-you-get editor; although, because it is not practical to see the actual data, you see only the editable version, along with the skeleton showing how the data will be generated.

To see what you would get in a report, you should check the **Preview** tab. It does not show the entire data, but shows the data as it will appear in the report and hides the way the report is generated (from the layout and the master page). There are some parts that do not get properly rendered, for example, the SVG images (although those will be rendered when the report is generated with an emitter supporting SVG).

Before each preview, the report design is saved.

On the **Master Page** tab, you can specify the header and footer for the report. By default, a KNIME-specific footer is there; you can remove/replace it if you want to use that space for a different purpose. You can also change the report page's size and orientation via its properties.

 Multiple master pages

You can create different master pages for the same report design to format different sections of the document with the corresponding header and footer, page size, margin, and orientation. To switch between the master pages, select one of the report items' properties in **General | Page Break**.

In the **XML Source** tab, you can fine tune the report design or check how it appears in a low-level description; however, the most important use case might be that of pasting parts from other designs so you do not have to go through all the options to change an element. You can also use this to correct misspellings and similar tasks with the **Find/Replace** dialog (*Ctrl + F*).

In visible views

We already mentioned that keeping the **KNIME Explorer** view is not so efficient. Here, you will get some tips on what should be visible to be more effective using the report editor.

The **Data Explorer** view gives an overview on not just data sources, sets, and cubes, but also on report parameters and variables. From its context menu, you can open dialogs to create and edit different entities of the tree.

There is an even more detailed view of the report design, the **Outline** view in **General**. It is so useful to navigate between the different parts of the report design and find out the parent/child relationships, that it is highly recommended to make it visible at least as a quick view.

The **Problems** view in **General** can also be useful for easily navigating to the errors and getting detailed information about them.

The **Report and Chart Design** category in the **Other...** view contains examples for more complex charts and reports with preview images. These views are **Chart Examples** and **Report Examples**. Unfortunately, neither of them supports an easy copy and paste or simple dragging option in this version of BIRT, although you can export the charts as an XML (using the icon with the arrow pointing upwards); add a new chart to your layout and replace its content in the **XML Source** tab of the editor with the content of the example chart.

With **Report Examples**, you can open or export the report design using the context menu, but neither of them is really a good option. If you select **Open**, you will get an error message because the generated project is not a workflow—so KNIME cannot handle it properly—but you can explore the different settings and check the XML version of it to copy the relevant parts. When you export, you can only use the XML version and select parts that are interesting for you blindly. A good compromise would be to have a separate Eclipse workspace with BIRT installed; open the reports you want to use for inspiration from there and copy the parts you find useful in the XML form from that instance. This way you will not get errors; you do not have to worry about potentially selecting something that you do not want.

Report properties

The report has some properties that should be introduced to be able to work efficiently with the designer. You can select a part of the page with no report item, and the properties view will show the available options.

The most common options are also available from the context menu, for example, the layout preference (fixed or auto), theme selection, or style handling.

The title, author, and other parameters can also be set in properties. To access them, you can use a code similar to the following statement from scripts:

```
reportContext.getDesignHandle().getProperty("title")
```

Let's go through what we have. The reportContext value holds the content associated with the report, and its design handle (getDesignHandle()) is responsible for the design time context. It has a getProperty method which can be used to get the values of a named property. How do we know how the properties are named? You can check the Javadoc of the associated class at the link:

```
http://help.eclipse.org/indigo/index.jsp?topic=%2Forg.eclipse.birt.
doc.isv%2Fengine%2Fapi%2Forg%2Feclipse%2Fbirt%2Freport%2Fengine%2Fapi
%2FIReportRunnable.html
```

On the other hand, to access the user properties or named expressions, you need the following object:

```
reportContext.getReportRunnable().getDesignInstance()
```

This is similar to the design handle discussed previously, but this is more like its runtime view. From this design instance, you can get not just the named expressions (the `getNamedExpression` method), the user properties (with the `getUserPropertyExpression` or the deprecated `getUserProperty` methods) but also the report items, styles, theme, and so on.

Report items

We will discuss the report items in this section in a bit more detail, because they have an important role on how the resulting report will look. We will only cover the items available in the default installation, but you can install others too.

You can insert report items either from **Palette** or from the **Insert** menu.

Each report item has properties, and most of them have the **Highlights** options for conditional formatting of texts. Only the **Chart** items miss this option. For **Image** items, only the alternative text can be formatted this way. You can apply a predefined style or use custom formatting.

The user properties and the named expressions are common properties for report items.

The comment and the visualization-related options (padding, margin, border, page break, visibility, localization, bookmark, and table of contents) are also common properties, just like the event handler, where you can specify a Java class from the libraries.

Label

With **Label,** you can show static text with various formatting for the whole text.

Text

The **Text** report item is quite similar to the **Label** item, although you can use formatting inside the item too. So, you do not need to break the text to multiple **Label** items.

To use dynamic text (result of a script), you can use the `<value-of>...</value-of>` tags.

When there are other report items or data set bind, you can use the expression builder's **Available Column Bindings** item.

Binding

This is the first report item in our list that has binding options, so we will introduce these options now.

You can bind certain report elements to either other report items or to data sets, although both have to be named (for data sets naming is usually done automatically). After binding, you can refer to the columns associated with the data set or the report item in the expressions.

> You can always bind to a newly created (not necessarily visible) **Table** instead of a KNIME data set; if you remove the original KNIME **Data to Report** or **Image to Report** node and use a compatible one, you have to change it only in a single place (in **Table**).

Without bindings, you should use global variables and custom code, so it's worth using bindings when applicable.

Dynamic text

When you need to generate a single text, you should use the **Dynamic Text** report item. It allows you to execute scripts to get the preferred content, not just to highlight the content on certain conditions. It also supports formatting within text, so it is more like the **Text** item and not like **Label**. However you can select the content type to be **Plain** (instead of **HTML**) to prevent further processing or adding text effects.

The main difference between **Text** and **Dynamic Text** is that the former requires to have `<value-of>` ... `</value-of>` blocks around the dynamic content, and the latter works the opposite way—you have to concatenate the static text to the dynamic content.

Data

Using the **Data** report items is a bit tricky. The following statement is a quote from its description:

Insert a Data Set column or expression result.

These are two different ways to represent data. When you grab it from **Palette** to a report design area, no bindings will be set by default, so you can only use other expressions. Although when you grab a column from **Data Explorer**, **Data set view**, or from the **Outline** view, you get the data to bind.

The binding options in the **Data** report item are the same as in other items. Although here you also have a **Map** tab in the **Property Editor** view where you can change the displayed values based on certain conditions—you can also use localization and use keys for translations.

Image

You can show images from four different sources: from a URI, from a shared resource folder (be careful when you export because you can select images from any KNIME project, not just the opened ones), from an embedded (in the report design xml) image, or a dynamic image.

You can also set the binding, so each row in a table can have the correct image displayed.

It is important to set the mime type of the image properly, such as image/png or image/svg+xml. This should be set in **Type Expression** (between quotes, as that expression is a JavaScript expression) in the **Advanced** property.

It is always a good habit to set a meaningful alternative text (**Alt Text**) to them, so the screen readers and potential robots can have an idea of what is on the image.

Grid

This is just a tool to arrange certain report items visually. It does not support binding, but you can format the grid lines.

List

When you want to represent the data in a single column, the **List** report item is a good choice. You can specify what should be in the header, footer, and detail. You can also define grouping of the data; this way, you can have something like tables in a table.

The column/group headers are typically the name of the content, but the detail is the actual data. The footer (and the group footer) can be used to show aggregate data, such as totals.

You can also change the values and their style based on conditions in the **Map** and **Highlights** tabs.

Because you can use grouping, you have a new tab named **Groups** in **Property Editor** for **List**, and you have an **Add Aggregation...** button below the **Add...** button on the **Binding** tab.

Groups

With groups, you can embed a range of values in the table, based on certain key values.

There are various options to set for each group; here is a screenshot of the new group dialog:

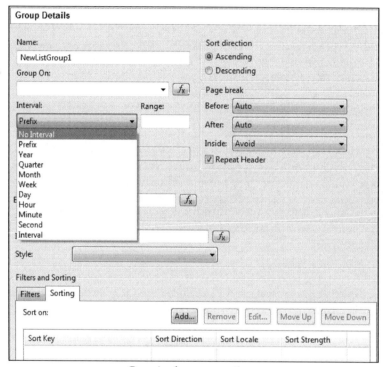

Grouping has many options

As you can see, you can sort the group values and the details within the group, but you can filter certain values too.

The interesting options are time-related grouping settings. It is not so easy to group data by time intervals within KNIME but in the report, you have a lot of options to do that.

Sorting

When you get the data, you do not necessarily have it in the right order, or you might not want to pass the same data with multiple sorting. For this reason you can sort the data based on the columns you prefer. This can be done by setting the preferences available on the **Sorting** tab. You can sort by multiple columns, and you can specify the locale and the strength. For details about the strength parameter, you should check the following page:

http://docs.oracle.com/javase/7/docs/api/java/text/Collator.
html#PRIMARY

Filters

Similar to sorting, you might need different subsets of the same data on different parts of the report, so it is useful to have an option to filter these values. On the **Filters** page, you can add filtering expressions to the data.

Table

The **Table** report items work similarly to the **List** items; the main difference is that it can handle multiple columns. You can set the headers, footers, the data, and the groups just like in the **List** item. All the other options available for them are available for **Table** items as well.

When you grab a data set from one of the contained views, you will get a **Table** with its content prefilled with the data set values.

Chart

As the adage says, "A picture is worth a thousand words," so it worth adding some figures and charts to the report to make it easier to understand it.

The following screenshot shows the available chart types:

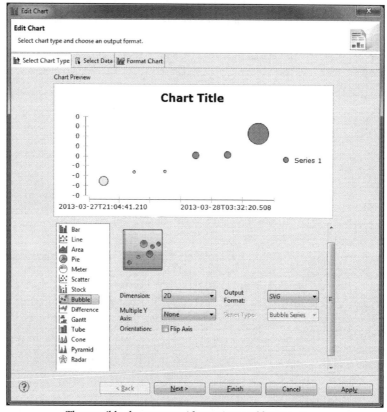

The possible chart types with preview and basic options

As you can see, some of the chart types have properties like that of subtype (this example has no other subtypes), dimension (**2D** or **2D With Depth**—parallel projection—or **3D**—perspective projection), and the output format. You can also specify the behavior of the series, and flip the axis.

New chart types can be added by using extensions. Most of the available chart types in the default installation might be familiar to you, although the **Gantt** and the **Meter** types are different from the previous options. The usual chart types also offer other subtypes that might be interesting for you.

When it comes to customization of charts, it gets as detailed as what the JFreeChart nodes offer. You can set each series and axis, just like the text and the background.

With a chart, you also have the option to highlight it on certain conditions, and to bind, filter, sort, or group the data in that chart.

Cross Tab

The last report item available in the default install is **Cross Tab**. It is designed to be used with a data cube, so you will need a data cube, although the designer can automatically generate it for you based on the data set you selected.

The **Cross Tab** report item looks similar to the **Table/Grid** items, analogous to the tables. When you drag a data cube to the report design area, a **Cross Tab** will be generated, not a **Table**.

Property Editor has some new tabs, the **Row Area** and the **Column Area**. These can be used to generate grand totals of the summarized values or subtotals when the splitting dimension is hierarchical. You can also influence the page breaks in these tabs.

The **Binding**, **Map**, **Highlights**, **Sorting**, and **Filters** tabs are similar in function and their appearance to the options similar in **Table**.

It is a bit hard to change the settings after the construction, so it is worth taking care when you create it. We will give you some help on how to change them if you are not satisfied with the results.

Setting up

Let's see how we can configure an empty **Cross Tab**. First, the group dimension of the cube should go to the rows or to the columns. You can select a different group to the other dimension if you prefer, but it is optional—both directions support hierarchical groups too.

> Use the rows when the group dimension has many different values, because usually the vertical space is less limited than the horizontal; although, the language of the report might prefer the other option. It is worth noting that there are the *birt-controls-lib* (`https://code.google.com/a/eclipselabs.org/p/birt-controls-lib/`) report items, where one of them is a rotated text. It might be useful for the columns.

When you are not using a predefined cube (for example, when you drag columns there from a data set), a cube creation wizard will open, where you can specify the groups and summary fields.

Next, you should add the summarized values to the **Drop data fields to be summarized here** cell by dragging them there from the **Data Explorer** or the **Outline** view.

Changing

Now, it is time to show the options to change the **Cross Tab** report items. Look at this simple **Cross Tab**:

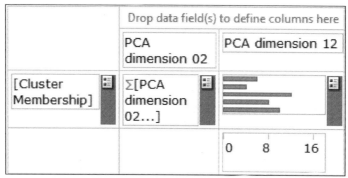

Design view of a Cross Tab report item

As you can see, the rows are showing the **Cluster Membership** values (this cube was created from a table generated by the KNIME **Data Generator** node and PCA transformed), but the columns do not split the data into groups.

In the summarized data section, there are two dimensions, one of them is created from *PCA dimension 0* and the other is from *PCA dimension 1*. The latter is represented by a chart, and the former is printed as text.

As you can see, all the row values and the summarized data cells have a gray bar with an icon to the right of them—the columns would also have one. The context menu of these areas gives you the option to change the preferences.

In the row or column, you have the following options (in the context menu): **Show/ Hide Group Levels**, **Totals**, and **Remove**. Because only a single cube dimension can be selected (for each row or column split area), the last one is most important from the modification point of view. Once you have removed the group, you can drag another group there just like we described in the previous section.

When you have hierarchical (typically time related) dimensions in the groups, the other two options will be useful too. By default, only the outer hierarchy is selected for the groups, but you can show the inner dimensions too with the **Show/Hide Group Levels** option.

Now, you might have an idea of what **Totals** might do. You can define the subtotals (based on inner dimensions) and the grand totals for each dimension (either rows or columns). You can do this on a well-designed interface. The former and later positions refer to the position relative to the summarized data.

In the summarized field, you have other options in the context menu. These are **Show as Text**, **Show as Chart**, **Add Relative Time Period**, **Add Derived Measure**, **Show/Hide Measures**, and **Remove**.

You can switch between the text and chart representation for each summarization separately. When you select a chart view, you can configure that chart from its context menu. The available chart types are: **Bar**, **Line**, **Area**, **Scatter**, **Tube**, **Cone**, and **Pyramid**. Each of these is represented by a single subtype.

Add Relative Time Period will be covered in the *Quick Tools* section soon.

With the **Add Derived Measure** menu item, the cube will not be affected; you can compute additional summarized values, but that is only visible in the **Cross Tab**.

The **Show/Hide Measures** allows you to select the summarized values you want to show, while the **Remove** item removes all the summarized values so you can drag other fields there.

Finally you can change the data cube you bind in the **Binding** tab in **Property Editor** of **Cross Tab**, which will clear all the previous bindings.

Using data cubes

You might already have cubes if you tried to grab a column from a data set to a **Cross Tab** report item; however, if you do not have a cube, you can create one from the context menu of the **Data Cubes** tree item in the **Data Explorer** or the **Outline** view.

In the data cube's context menu, you can select the **Edit** option, or simply double-clicking on it will bring up the configuration dialog. Here you can change the associated data set, and add, change, or remove summary fields or groups. For dates, you have two group options: the first is creating regular groups or time groups, and the latter is the recommended option, because a hierarchy will be automatically created for the date/time.

There is also an option to link to other data sets and set the dimensions that should be used to join them in the **Link Groups** tab.

Handling dates

Because you cannot group by a newly defined computed column, you must be sure that the initial data set's column is not a string, but has a date or datetime type. You can create new columns for the dates in the data set with the compute column option.

Quick Tools

The **Quick Tools** option offers shortcuts to common tasks.

Aggregation

In the **Aggregation** dialog, you can easily add aggregated data to the footers of a **Table**. For example, there is no need to calculate a new column and bind to that; just drag the **Aggregation** item to the place where you need a single value generated from a data set, and use the dialog to set the parameters.

The **Aggregation** items do not support data cubes, and you cannot use another data set for computation. This reduces the chance to show something unrelated to the data set.

Be careful about copying the aggregations around as — unlike Excel — the report designer will not adjust the columns according to the position. It is recommended to configure each aggregation independently, and not copy them.

Relative time period

The **Relative Time Period** item is applicable only if at least one of the group dimensions is temporal. Just drag it to the summary data area, and the dialog will guide you through the new column configuration. Alternatively, you can select the **Add Relative Time Period** option from a summarized column's context menu.

The cube will not get changed, but you will be able to show the data in **Cross Tab** compared to historical data, for example.

Configuring the time period is straightforward. You have to select the expression (usually a measure) to summarize by the selected time period (it has many options, such as previous *n* years, current year, month to-date, last year, and so on) and select the aggregation function. You can also select a reference date and filter the data, the time dimension, and the aggregation dimensions.

This way, you can create complex tables without the need to do a lot of scripting.

Generating reports

At the end, the goal is to have a nice document with all the data transformed according to the report design.

To export `rptdocument` (the report document), navigate to **Run | Generate Document**. This way, you will be able to use this in other frameworks compatible with BIRT, such as a report server. For details check the BIRT integration guide:

`http://www.eclipse.org/birt/phoenix/deploy/`

When you want to export the report in a more static format, you should select one of the options in **Run | View Report,** or use the icon that resembles "Earth" from the icon's menu to access the same options. The default installation has the following options to export the document: *Web Viewer* (it is an interactive local or remote report viewer), doc, HTML, odp, ods, odt, pdf, postscript, ppt, and xls.

> The ppt support is not ideal; visit the following link for more information:`https://bugs.eclipse.org/bugs/show_bug.cgi?id=328982`

When you either generate or just view the report, you will be prompted for the report parameters. You can specify them in the URL. For further details, please refer to `http://www.eclipse.org/birt/phoenix/deploy/viewerUsage.php#parameters`.

Different emitters have different capabilities, so it worth testing all the export options you want to support on a sample data.

Similar to many other parts of BIRT and KNIME, there are additional extensions for exports too; search for them with the BIRT emitter search expression.

Using colors

There are a few KNIME example workflows on the public server; in this section, we just mention one of them, which describes how to use the color information present in KNIME in the reports.

The **010006_UseKNIMEColorsInReporting** workflow is available from the KNIME public server. To use it, just copy it from the public server and paste it to the local workspace.

It requires a basic scripting knowledge, but the workflow gives detailed description on how to use the color information so that it can be used as an introduction to scripting.

If you are fine not defining the colors in the KNIME workflow, it might be easier to define those within the reporting template and bind the colors to certain values.

Using HiLite

There is no direct option to handle the HiLite information within the report, but you can easily work around this.

First, you can add a new table where you have the highlighted rows filtered by the **HiLite Filter** node. This way, you need to use this other table to signal (for example, with highlights) what was "HiLited". This has an advantage, in that it does not require manual steps, but it might be a good idea to add a new column to the result and rejoin it with the original table before sending the data to the report editor.

Another option is using **Interactive HiLite Collector**. Its output can contain different information based on different groups. So in the reporting data, you can choose between multiple visualizations; you can even combine them. The drawback is that it requires to be set manually after each reset of the node with the same column names/values.

Using workflow variables

The following video link demonstrates how you can create a workflow with parameters set for the workflow but still used in the report generation:

`http://youtu.be/RHvVuHsvf0U`

Basically, the recipe is to create a workflow variable with a name and type you want to use in the report. This workflow variable will appear in the report designer as a report parameter.

If you use the workflow variable in the workflow in a way that can change the data passed to the report generating engine (in the example, the data was filtered according its value), you can use this variable as a report parameter and generate the report with the updated data.

In the example, it is also demonstrated that you can pass another table to the report generator, and use that information to set the domain of the possible values for that report parameter. This might be an unexpected way to parameterize your execution, but it is a quite powerful option. You can check this behavior using our example workflow from the `workflowVariables.zip` file.

Suggested readings

In this chapter, we have covered the basics, but the BIRT ecosystem has much more to offer. The most important might be the way you can create interactive reports. Although there are highly interactive components available, such as the BIRT Interactive Viewer (`http://www.birt-exchange.com/be/products/birt-user-experience/interactive-viewer/features/`), which is not an open source option, you still have the option to change the behavior on certain conditions with JavaScript.

The *Advanced BIRT Report Customization: Report Scripting* video (from 2008) might be a good start towards scripting. You can view it after registration at the following link:

`http://www.birt-exchange.com/be/info/birtscripting-websem/`

There is a nice JavaScript library named D3.js (`http://d3js.org`), which allows you to have reports almost as interactive as the BIRT Interactive Viewer would offer for certain output formats. An example on how you can combine both BIRT and D3.js together can be found at `http://www.birt-exchange.org/org/devshare/designing-birt-reports/1535-d3-tree-node-layout-example/`.

You can check the other KNIME workflows featuring KNIME reporting; it can help you get familiarized with how to use both parts of KNIME efficiently, and which tasks should be done in separate processing steps.

If you prefer, you can check the following YouTube videos from the KNIME documentation page (`http://tech.knime.org/screencasts-0`):

- *KNIME Report Creation*: `http://youtu.be/jKWQhFrBuzQ`
- *KNIME - Use of Variables with Reporting*: `http://youtu.be/RHvVuHsvf0U`
- *KNIME - Including Chemical Structures in Reporting*: `http://youtu.be/5T2SIrKAc5s`

The BIRT Exchange site (`http://www.birt-exchange.org/org/home/`) is also a great source of help. It contains tutorials, examples, and components. Obviously, the Eclipse BIRT home page (`http://www.eclipse.org/birt/phoenix/`) can also be a good place to start.

The other user communities (for example, `http://www.birtreporting.com`) and BIRT-related materials are usually easily adaptable for KNIME reporting. If you do not find a solution for your KNIME reporting problem, it is always a good strategy to try it with the *BIRT* search expression instead of *KNIME reporting*.

The companies offering commercial extensions for BIRT usually also have some BIRT-related forums or articles.

If you want to integrate the reporting to another product, the *Jason Weathersby; Tom Bondur;* and *Iana Chatalbasheva's* book *Integrating and Extending BIRT* may be interesting for you.

Finally, you can read the following two books that might be useful for digging deep into the BIRT design:

- *BIRT A Field Guide* by *Diana Peh, Nola Hague,* and *Jane Tatchell*
- *Practical Data Analysis and Reporting with BIRT* by *John Ward*

Summary

In this chapter we introduced how to import data to KNIME Report Designer (we also covered the installation). The main concepts were explained before we went through the basics of report design. Before we gave some examples on how this can be used in practice, we also presented how you can export your documents. Finally, we suggested some further learning materials, because this chapter is just the surface of what you can achieve with KNIME and BIRT.

Index

U

Ungroup node 43
unpivoting 44
use cases, HiLite 83
User Interface
about 17
extensions, installing 18
setting preferences 17
workbench 19, 20

V

Value Counter node 68
values, transforming
conversion between types 49, 50
generic transformations 46
multiple columns 53, 54
normalization 51
smoothing 55
time transformation 54, 55
XML transformation 54
variable flows 26
views
visual guide 72
visualization nodes
about 92
HiTS visualization 94
Matlab plot 93
official R plots 93
Python plot 93
RapidMiner view 93
R plot 93
visualizations
overview 70-72
visual properties
color property 80
shape property 81
size property 81
using 80

W

Web-Harvest
URL 54
web services
data, importing from 33, 34
whole match
versus partial match 38
WIKIDATA
URL 35
wildcard patterns 39
Windows
KNIME, installing for 8, 9
Windows Azure Marketplace
URL 35
workbench
meta nodes 26
node controls 22-25
workflow, handling 21, 22
workflow lifecycle 26, 27
workflow customization 61, 62
Workflow Editor 10
workflow groups 10
workflow lifecycle 26, 27
workflow variables
using 122

X

XML files
importing 34
XML transformation 54

Y

YAGO2
URL 35

Z

Z-score normalization 51

Thank you for buying
KNIME Essentials

About Packt Publishing

Packt, pronounced 'packed', published its first book "*Mastering phpMyAdmin for Effective MySQL Management*" in April 2004 and subsequently continued to specialize in publishing highly focused books on specific technologies and solutions.

Our books and publications share the experiences of your fellow IT professionals in adapting and customizing today's systems, applications, and frameworks. Our solution based books give you the knowledge and power to customize the software and technologies you're using to get the job done. Packt books are more specific and less general than the IT books you have seen in the past. Our unique business model allows us to bring you more focused information, giving you more of what you need to know, and less of what you don't.

Packt is a modern, yet unique publishing company, which focuses on producing quality, cutting-edge books for communities of developers, administrators, and newbies alike. For more information, please visit our website: www.packtpub.com.

Writing for Packt

We welcome all inquiries from people who are interested in authoring. Book proposals should be sent to author@packtpub.com. If your book idea is still at an early stage and you would like to discuss it first before writing a formal book proposal, contact us; one of our commissioning editors will get in touch with you.

We're not just looking for published authors; if you have strong technical skills but no writing experience, our experienced editors can help you develop a writing career, or simply get some additional reward for your expertise.

MATLAB Graphics and
Data Visualization Cookbook

Tell data stories with compelling graphics using this collection of
data visualization recipes

Nivedita Majumdar
Swapnonil Banerjee

MATLAB Graphics and Data Visualization Cookbook

ISBN: 978-1-84969-316-5   Paperback: 284 pages

Tell data stories with compelling graphics using this collection of data visualization recipes

1. Collection of data visualization recipes with functionalized versions of common tasks for easy integration into your data analysis workflow

2. Recipes cross-referenced with MATLAB product pages and MATLAB Central File Exchange resources for improved coverage

3. Includes hand created indices to find exactly what you need; such as application driven, or functionality driven solutions

Data Visualization:
a successful design
process

Andy Kirk   PACKT

Data Visualization: a successful design process

ISBN: 978-1-84969-346-2   Paperback: 206 pages

A structured design approach to equip you with the knowledge if how to successfully accomplish any data visualization challenge efficiently and effectively

1. A portable, versatile and flexible data visualization design approach that will help you navigate the complex path towards success

2. Explains the many different reasons for creating visualizations and identifies the key parameters which lead to very different design options

3. Thorough explanation of the many visual variables and visualization taxonomy to provide you with a menu of creative options

Please check **www.PacktPub.com** for information on our titles

Circos Data Visualization How-to

ISBN: 978-1-84969-440-7   Paperback: 72 pages

Create dynamic data visualizations in the social, physical, and computer science with the Circos data visualization program

1. Learn something new in an Instant! A short, fast, focused guide delivering immediate results.

2. Transform simple tables into engaging diagrams

3. Learn to install Circos on Windows, Linux, and MacOS

4. Create Circos diagrams using ribbons, heatmaps, and other data tracks

Learning IPython for Interactive Computing and Data Visualization

ISBN: 978-1-78216-993-2   Paperback: 138 pages

Learn IPython for interactive Python programming, high-performance numerical computing, and data visualization

1. A practical step-by-step tutorial which will help you to replace the Python console with the powerful IPython command-line interface

2. Use the IPython notebook to modernize the way you interact with Python

3. Perform highly efficient computations with NumPy and Pandas

4. Optimize your code using parallel computing and Cython

Please check **www.PacktPub.com** for information on our titles

42010265R00083

Made in the USA
Lexington, KY
04 June 2015